The Eurasian Miracle

The Eurasian Miracle

Jack Goody

polity

Contents

1

Alternation or supremacy?

A short introduction to a short book. This book is about the relative unity of the European and Asian continents rather than their differences, a relative unity that began with the Bronze Age Revolution. That great change – what the pre-historian Gordon Childe has described as the beginning of the Culture of Cities (hence Civilization in his sense) – did not result in a bifurcation between the dynamic west, passing through antiquity, and feudalism, to capitalism, and the east that produced a static, hydraulic, bureaucratic, despotism, which was not about to modernize. This was the nineteenth-century theory of the earlier sociologists, Marx, Weber and many European historians, who saw the world from the standpoint of Europe's predominance and presumed it had always had an advantage. No one is doubting the achievements of Europe in the Industrial Revolution, nor yet in the Renaissance. What is at stake is the extent to which this was European. In some respects its roots were Eurasian, but in any case the key movement is alternation between post-Bronze Age societies, rather than viewing one as having a permanent advantage over the other.

This first chapter attempts to deal with various Europeanist arguments that propose a completely different trajectory in the west. It is based upon my contribution to a conference

The Eurasian Miracle

held in Cambridge in September 1985 under the title of 'The European Miracle'. On this occasion I began to query the whole discussion on the grounds that it placed too much emphasis on the invention of something called 'capitalism', it neglected the contributions of other societies to the achievements of the Industrial Revolution and, in particular, it overlooked the contributions of the east to 'modernization', mechanization and industrialization. The thesis of the book was not wrong in recognizing the advantage gained by the west after the Renaissance and especially in the nineteenth century after the Industrial Revolution, but it seemed to be an example of ethnocentric teleology in so far as it attributed that European achievement to deep-rooted, quasi-permanent features of the west, rather than recognizing the phenomenon of alternation of advantage in an exchange economy (which included the exchange of information).

This short book contains little that I have not hinted at before but much that I wanted to clarify – and, specifically, the aspect of alternation among the major civilizations of Eurasia, which raises the question of why I think the so-called 'European miracle' was part of a wider Eurasian phenomenon, developing as it did in the nineteenth century (and even before in the Renaissance), but also of why I cannot agree with the kind of essentialist account that Europeans have been only too ready to offer. Alternation automatically rejects essentialism and the notion of permanent advantage.

The idea for this book came from John Thompson who pointed out that I needed to deal more specifically with the question of 'why capitalism in Europe?' That made me look again at the report of the conference, which only confirmed my belief that capitalism had to be seen in a wider Eurasian context where there were a succession of miracles and rebirths. What happened in Europe in the sixteenth and nineteenth centuries was part of these. Today we are experiencing another swing towards the east, which is not simply copying the west but picking up on earlier achievements. Only such a hypothesis can explain the different records of development in Asia and in Africa, which never experienced

2

the Bronze Age Revolution. The foundation of the culture of cooking and the growth of a 'grand cuisine' as well as the culture of flowers are things I constantly refer to, partly because these are areas in which I have done extensive research.[1]

But also they are areas outside the normal range of economic purview, even though they were much influenced by the economy, and they are areas associated with more general cultural achievement. Nevertheless, as I have argued, they are areas in which the west remained in constant comparison with the east, which in many respects had the advantage over a long period, so that neither the economy nor the knowledge system was inferior to that of the west.

2

Why European and not Eurasian?

It was is the 1980s that a number of European intellectuals – Jean Baechler, John Hall and Michael Mann – held a prestigious conference where proceedings were published as a book on the European Miracle. It dealt with the particular ideological or political structures of the east and west. That is to say, it dealt with the twin questions of the 'uniqueness of the west' and 'the miracle of the west' that not only have formed the central focus of enquiry explicitly in the works of Marx, Weber and countless other economists, sociologists and historians, but are implicitly subsumed by the folk-models of most Europeans and in the analytic categories of those anthropologists, and other scholars, who draw a broad black line between modern and traditional, industrial and pre-industrial, advanced and primitive, indeed between 'we' and 'they'.

It was on this latter point that I disagreed with the bulk of Europeanists since I saw many of the arguments put forward by them – including Marx and Weber, and the historians, Braudel, Laslett and Joseph Needham – as being mistaken, indeed teleological. I do not want to rehearse these arguments now except briefly to mention the thesis, central to the work of the whole Cambridge Group in population studies which Laslett headed, that the 'European marriage pattern' (of the statistician John Haynal) was singular in promoting a late marriage age for men and women, which meant that they had fewer children and more Weberian restraint (part of the Protestant ethic), following the late eighteenth-century comments of the Revd Malthus. The Chinese on the other hand married earlier and were less constrained in their sexual life, producing more and more offspring. The thesis was obviously in tune with the work of Max Weber and the importance of the Protestant ethic in the establishment of capitalism in the west and the supposed 'failure' of the east to achieve it.

In the eyes of many Europeans, a fundamental difference of this kind went back long before the rise of capitalism, to antiquity itself (which apparently only occurred in the west) and indeed to the division, so critical to Marx and many others, between an east characterized by authoritarian rule and by the Asiatic mode of production and the west with its slave society in Greece and Rome leading to the emergence of feudalism and then of capitalism.

While my own speciality of social anthropology in no way depends upon the nature of these modes of production, nevertheless it reinforced in many minds a binary division between east and west, the traditional and the modern. For instance, the French sociologists Durkheim and Mauss included China in their analysis of 'primitive classification'; the French anthropologist Lévi-Strauss cited the Chinese as an example of cross-cousin marriage in his 'Elementary Forms of Kinship', just as his colleague, Dumont, contrasted India with Europe in his discussion of stratification. Yet how could we reconcile these discussions with the sinologist Needham's demonstration that, until the Renaissance, China was ahead of Europe as far as most science was concerned. In other words, Durkheim was taking a very partial view of the Chinese system of classification, denying it 'modernity' in the same way that Lévi-Strauss did for the kinship system when, following the French sinologist Granet, he speaks of a system of marriage which falls into his category of 'elementary forms'. But if Chinese kinship is elementary, then there must be queries about Europe too, since it had a similar system of dowry endowment as an aspect of marriage.[1] In fact, there are many other resemblances, but the Europeans have constantly attempted to point to the differences, to the supposed absence of the notion of love, to the early marriage and to the assumed plethora of children, especially in the work of Malthus who presumed a dramatic contrast between the two. Yes, they had early marriage, which inevitably limited individuals' choice of spouse, as many have shown, but they did not have the runaway family life that he supposed. While they started marrying and producing children earlier than in the west, their rate of marital fertility (children within marriage) was lower than Europe's, partly because the latter had no post-partum sex taboo and women could start procreating again straight away after a birth. My maternal grandmother had thirteen children, of which my mother was the last, and could have had little time for anything except childbearing and going to the kirk. Although in the west some may have exercised a Protestant restraint *before* marriage, despite the practice of 'bundling' (spending the night without penetration) and the incidence of pre-marital conception or even births, the Chinese practised limitation *within* marriage. One region of the globe was no more socially restrained than another, yet Europeans congratulated themselves on the uniqueness of this quality, which was supposed to be involved in the birth of capitalism, to which they also laid claim.

It is this same view of 'the uniqueness of the West' that has given rise to the ideas that love, at least romantic love, originated in Europe among the troubadours of twelfth-century Provence and that the bulk of unions in the west were 'love' marriages, as distinct from the arranged weddings of Asia (and, of course, the Near East, including the Jews, whom Sombart has seen as central to the birth of 'capitalism'). Provence, of course, was much influenced by Muslim Spain, where love poetry abounded, demonstrating that the European thesis had little value. It is true that late marriage, which was emphatically not the route chosen by Juliet in her liaison with Romeo, gave more scope for the choice of spouse, at least in first marriages. But divorce and remarriage (which was necessarily freer) were common features of Arab unions. In any case, even with arranged marriages, who is to say that parents make worse choices for young partners? Certainly this is delicate ground upon which to build a theory of difference.

There is a similar problem with the anthropologist Dumont's contrast between the class system of the west and the caste system of India. The first produced the essayist Mandeville as well as Marx, which gave him the title of his book *From Mandeville to Marx*; the latter, however, resisted the advent of modernity, differentiating Europe from Asia. From the African point of view, both systems are aspects of stratified societies built upon the complex civilization of the Bronze Age. No doubt the caste systems of India were more restrictive than the class systems of the west, but the differences should not be exaggerated. In the west too, certain tasks were confined to specific groups, within which marriage took place in endogamous unions. In-marriage, as the French historian Marc Bloch pointed out, was part of the way that sub-classes were formed. But it was not obligatory as in India; however, the difference between a stated norm (what people were supposed to do) and an actual practice was not all that great in its social consequences, and to regard one as embodying freedom and the other as constraint (as with marriage) is misleading, although the idea forms an important part of 'modern' western ideology. Certainly, one form of stratification may have been somewhat easier to bypass than the other – though, until recently, not as easy as is often thought.

There is also the question of timing; whereas Weber discusses the advent of Protestantism in the sixteenth century, raised in chapter 11 of the Miracle book, other authors have concerned themselves with features that were already present such as family structure, individualism, developments in the Graeco-Roman tradition (chapter 10 of that book) or in the wider Christian church that was supposed to have predisposed Europe, or a particular part of that continent, to be the cradle of industrial capitalism.

The Eurasian Miracle

The problem I had is best illustrated in chapters 3 and 4 below. It was not to deny the advantage that Europe and the USA had enjoyed since the nineteenth century, and in some ways since the Renaissance, but to see that this priority – especially with regard to the extensive production of cheap metal, to the mechanized factory production of commodities plus intellectual achievements – had nothing to do with primordial features that would have excluded others from participation (or at least inauguration). But it was also related to an alternation between interacting civilizations in Eurasia, in which first one, then the other, was privileged. So that there was no unique, unilineal transition from antiquity to feudalism to capitalism. The notion of antiquity referred to a type of Bronze Age society, possibly with a greater emphasis on slavery, but this institution was in no sense intrinsic to the above sequence. Nor yet was feudalism, which represented an effective decentralization of political and economic activity, a 'catastrophic regression' in the historian Perry Anderson's words. And, as Braudel realized, 'capitalism' in a broad sense (mercantile exchange) developed in the Bronze Age and continued to do so right up to the appearance of its industrial form.

The alternative position taken in the Miracle book, and by many others, is both essentialist and Eurocentric. It fails to take account of the alternation of post-Bronze Age culture within Eurasia and it is this position, which does not deny recent Euro-American advances, that I attempted to outline in my contribution to this conference, which was not included in the printed version, presumably because it was contrary to the organizers' beliefs.

These arguments (see appendix 1), put forward by those I shall refer to as Europeanists, are problematic in several senses. Since they are largely self-congratulary, that is, viewed from the standpoint of those who see themselves as benefitting from the miracle – indeed bringing it about – they are in the first instance directed internally, looking for factors unique to Europe, to western Europe, to north-western Europe, or even, in some cases, to England. There are clearly two pitfalls in this approach, related to the argument's ethnocentric point of departure: namely, the pitfalls of overestimating the uniqueness and of overestimating the miracle.

One result of the first of these is that scholars look around the world in an attempt to discern critical differences in other major civilizations, thereby discovering the stagnant quality of Asiatic systems or the non-compatibility of the economic ethic of Islam or of Hinduism. While the desire for comparison is to be applauded, this particular enterprise is focused entirely around the question of 'why did the Oriental civilizations fail to develop capitalism?'. What were 'the unique characteristics' of western civilization that led to its rise?[2]

A consequence of the second of these pitfalls is the tendency to overstate the nature of the leap-forward at any particular moment in time, a point that is illustrated in the problems facing scholars in deciding when those critical transformations took place. Some see 'real capitalism' as the industrial capitalism of the late eighteenth century.[3] Others see mercantile capitalism as following the dissolution of feudal Europe; yet others search for proto-capitalism at an earlier period, in simpler conditions, even among African cultivators. More traditionally, Guy Bois writes of the period between 1300 and 1500 as being the one in which the feudal mode of production declined, simultaneously with the rise of capitalism[4] – in other words the period before the expansion of Europe either towards the New World or to India and the East Indies, the expansion of mercantile and of booty production. Yet it is not clear that 'capitalism' provided the Spanish and Portuguese conquerors of the New World with any great superiority to the conquered, certainly not morally or ethically, except that they had the ships, the horses and the swords, and, later on, muskets and writing itself were additional advantages. In India, virtually the only initial advantages of the Europeans were their improved clocks and guns.

What has happened here? A series of transformations extended over time are summed up as the shift from one designated state of the world to another, from feudalism to capitalism. I do not argue for a gradualist rather than a revolutionary or cataclysmic approach; however, the way the transition is phrased tends to identify certain sets of social relations with certain systems of production or polity *in an exclusive manner*. For many purposes this tendency turns out to be simplistic, reinforcing the ideas both of uniqueness and of the miracle. For a much earlier period, the consequent problems are clearly raised in discussions about the nature of Assyrian trade as early as the nineteenth century BCE and before – in which attempts to deny the presence and importance of entrepreneurs, of money and of the market (even at selected moments in history and even in forms admittedly different from later ones) appear to over-emphasize the differences and to 'primitivize' not only the ancient economy but the ancient world as a whole.[5] The same tendency is present in the search for anthropological parallels for the rituals of ancient Greece among the Australian aborigines (e.g. in the admirable work of the Cambridge classicists Cornford and Harrison), neglecting their affinities with contemporary initiation rites of the Masonic order or the procedures of the mass.

This tendency is illustrated by reference to a fascinating and learned article by the geographer Wheatley, on trade in south-east Asia, in a volume called *Ancient Civilization and Trade*.[6] The contribution, which suggests how the overseas trade of Indian merchants undermined the structure of societies in the peninsula, leading to their subsequent 'brahmanization', is subtitled 'from reciprocity to redistribution'. These categories of exchange are, of course, much used in anthropology and cultural history, being given currency in the valuable works of Karl Polanyi, whose substantive approach to the economy (markets were concrete institutions) represents, on the one hand, a rejection of classical economics and, on the other, a modification of Marxist and similar theories. Without intending to accept the application of all of classical economic theory to non-industrial economies, one might wonder whether, at least on one level, the commercial activities of the Christian European natives, who came as Portuguese into the Indian Ocean, were really so very different, at least in the initial stages, from those of the Arabs and Indians that preceded them. Different enough, that is to say, to exclude one from the category of 'trade' and the other from that of 'redistribution'.

In practice most scholars treat factors like money, redistribution, wage-labour, capitalistic activity, as variables present in a wide range of socio-economic systems, but as 'dominant' in certain forms. Once this is admitted, however, the problem of explanation takes on a very different shape and the question of the initiating factors of a miracle becomes a matter not so much of uniqueness but of range, of emphasis, or of percentage points.

There is another factor that suggests the need for a radical review. Now that the 'supremacy of western Europe' is threatened by the rapid industrialization of other parts of the world and is beginning to be seen to be of the short rather than of the long *durée*, a matter of a particular social organization rather than of general moral performance, it is worth looking again at some of the basic assumptions, to revaluate what needs to be explained before hunting round for an explanation. A sceptical approach to the European experience seems to be warranted by the number of different countries that are now contributing to industrial modernization and that look like outstripping the west in various ways in the near future, where they have not already done so. True, one can 'explain' this situation by asserting that initiation is one thing and development another. But that contention requires a belief in the validity of a radical distinction between the two rather than an interpretation of interpenetrating features, combined with certitude about one's periodization that a moment's reflection would lead one to doubt. In any case, much of the 'uniqueness' argument would imply the impossibility of such an economic transformation elsewhere before substantial changes in the rest of the mentality or social structure had taken place. The actual course of events in the contemporary Far East, as well as studies of earlier cultures, do not altogether confirm, for example, the special position of Protestantism with regard to entrepreneurial activity.[7] It is true that Catholicism, like Islam and Judaism, prohibited usury. But members of all three religions nevertheless practised mercantile activity, and ways around the prohibition were easily available.

I make this suggestion about revaluation in a programmatic way. The task will no doubt have to be finally accomplished by some historian from a non-western culture. But for the present discussion I offer some general remarks of the 'notes towards . . .' variety. These will be mainly geared to the economy since it is in these terms the transformation has usually been characterized, although in my own view an important element in the modernization of western Europe (and one rapidly adopted by other major civilizations who themselves had earlier made substantial contributions to these processes) lay in changes in the modes of communication as well as modes of production and transport, and in the shift to more secular ways of thinking and acting that were encouraged in the period of humanism or in the Renaissance, as well as before and elsewhere.

In thinking of the developments that took place in western Europe, we should remember the relative backwardness of that continent in the early medieval period, despite the fact that Roman civilization and the Christian religion had brought the benefits of the Mediterranean world, through which were also communicated many of the basic technological and some intellectual advances of the east, of Persia, India and China. Looking at medieval Europe, one author has characterized the differing socio-economic systems of Christian and Islamic Spain between the conquest in 615 and 1300 in the following words: 'One bloc, Islamic, dominant until the eleventh century, was an expanding, "urban-artisanal" society, fully implanted in a larger economic network. The other bloc, the Christian, was for most of the same period a heavily ruralised region which for the present we can characterise as "static-agrarian".'[8] As medievalists have increasingly insisted in recent years, the eleventh and twelfth centuries were a period of dynamic growth.[9] But then the starting point was in most respects far behind the major civilizations of Asia, a fact that is evident at the time of the first European contacts; writing of the advent of the Europeans to the Indian Ocean in the sixteenth century, the American historian Pearson notes the relatively small initial impact that they had.[10]

While the nature of the labour force is a critical feature of all political economies, I do not accept the notion that the dominance of a particular relationship was an absolute bar to – though it might inhibit the adoption of – other forms, or even of industrial types of production. Most societies have a mix of labour farms, which open up many possibilities. Let us take the case of Africa in recent times. Before 1900 there was effectively no 'free' labour market in northern Ghana. Under hoe agriculture in acephalous societies, people laboured on each other's farms at certain times of the year, largely but not entirely on a reciprocal basis: they were rewarded with food and drink, the ingredients for which the farmer might have to purchase with cowries in the local market. If, in the centralized kingdom of the area, a chief called for such help, there was an obligation to assist that was certainly not reciprocated in the same terms. It is arguable that it was reciprocated by help in other ways, although the line between exploitation and reciprocity is often a shadowy one. In addition there was some slave labour, as well as a vigorous trade in cloth and kola nuts and other commodities. Mining for salt and precious metals was carried out both by individual entrepreneurs and by paid employees and slaves. A form of modernized production was carried out on the loom, with the product consumed locally and at a distance. Some labour was paid, or rewarded in a fashion. There was little problem when it came to working in the mines or on cocoa-farms in 'capitalistic' enterprises.[11]

Mercantile activity was widespread in earlier Africa – so, too, in India, in a more complex fashion. So was there something fundamental in Indian society – let us not confine ourself to the economy – that prevented the development of industrial production? Writing of the north of the continent during the Mughal period, the historian Raychauduri is

The Eurasian Miracle

tempted to speculate that the state industries producing for the court, the *karkhanas*, might have moved in the direction of mechanization and become state model factories for the modern industrialization of India, had they not been terminated by the British conquest.[12] This is speculation. But there are other aspects that point in a similar direction. 'The collection of revenue in cash helped to bind the remotest peasant to the network of exchange';[13] 'capitalistic features' in the trader–artisan relationship existed, though closely interwoven with earlier caste solidarity.

For the north of India, another historian, Chandra, notes the growth of a money economy under the Mughal regime of the seventeenth century. Extensive overseas trade had existed since much earlier times, and this involved production for export, based largely on the household economy but involving merchants and money-lenders, traders and bankers. Nor was this trade in any sense marginal. When the Europeans arrived in India, one of the merchants, with branches in a number of towns and chartering European ships, was reported to be the richest in the world.[14] They found a number of towns as big as, or bigger than, London or Paris. Mercantile capitalism, the money economy, production for the market, all were well developed, as was a thriving range of craft industries. However, the notion of growth of such activities at this period should be interpreted as 'expansion'. For while sales of land undoubtedly increased, they had existed for a long time before. So too the other features of the economy. It was the scale that increased.

What about production, as distinct from distribution? In the ancient Near East, industrial production existed only on a small scale and the economy was basically agricultural. Up to the Muslim Middle Ages, the orientalist Oppenheim claims, extra-household production was concerned with the weaving of textiles and related activities, but was carried out mainly in workshops of the 'great organizations'.[15] Elsewhere, it was more industrialized. The labour seems to have been partly slave, partly free. Later in the ancient world of Greece and Rome, workshops were initially often manned by slaves. In the Italy of Augustus, the flourishing potteries of Arezzo, producing the new *terra sigillata* (stamped ware), employed only slaves, the largest number known in a single establishment being fifty-eight.[16] When production moved to Gaul, it was carried on by independent craftsmen working in smaller enterprises with mainly free labour.[17] In the later Roman Empire, the state factories that were now engaged in the direct production of items such as the uniforms and weapons required by the armies utilized a workforce that was servile in a more general sense, the distinction between slavery and other forms of involuntary labour having almost disappeared. All these forms of labour were present.

In India things were not very different. While servile castes of Untouchables took part in the production of cloth, so did non-servile groups such as Shudras. Trade was in the hands of specialist groups of Muslims and Hindus of the *vanias* category, very numerous and active in Gujarat. It is true that, in terms of social hierarchy, they were lower in the religious scale than priests and warriors, let alone the rulers, but that did not appear greatly to inhibit their enterprise. Pearson remarks upon their adaptability in the face of the many different conditions under which they worked, being dynamic and open to new ideas.[18]

The same dynamism was found in manufacture. Just as the Chinese adopted decorative themes from abroad, incorporated them into porcelain designs and then modified these for the export market,[19] so too did the Indians with their cotton cloth. The attractions of printed cotton or chintz for the European market were such that British and Dutch merchants fed back information upon designs that would be popular in their materials, thus altering the content as well as the volume of that segment of the export industry and at the same time influencing internal taste.[20]

While early trade between India and Europe concentrated on spices and the cheaper pepper, mostly imported by the Portuguese and Dutch, it was not long before manufactured goods in the shape of textiles took over: 'From trading Coromandel and Gujarat piece-goods to the Indonesian archipelago, the European Companies found it an easy step to extend their import into Europe itself.'[21] First, small samples were brought to London; then in 1613 calico appears as a regular item in the Company's auction sales, the fine white fabrics being considered suitable for the 'Moorish' market and the painted calicos for fine quilts and wall hangings at home. These goods were able to compete because they were cheaper than local linen cloth, but other advantages of this more colourful material and design (cotton took colour better than linen or wool) were also important in the rapid increase of the sales to western Europe, which eventually led to the imposition of heavy protectionist duties in favour of home-produced silk in many countries. By 1684 the number of pieces of cloth imported by the English Company amounted to more than 1.5 million.

The local organization of cloth production on this scale meant a dramatic increase in the numbers involved. In Bengal in the early eighteenth century employment was provided for a sizeable section of the population and the income from taxes on merchants and weavers was considerable. Production was organized on the basis of a putting-out system, but one which usually involved not the supply of materials to the artisans but the provision of cash advances, which the merchants in turn obtained from the trading companies and which were regarded as a deposit on the orders.

In India, production and distribution were closely interlinked with the caste system. But this does not seem to entail as great a barrier as Weber and others supposed. Neither in the earlier nor in the later period can it be established that the caste system prevented the growth of entrepreneurial activity. Look, for example, at the traders (*baniva*) or at banking groups such as the Nattukottai Chattiar of southern India. Traditionally they traded in textiles and rice, developing what has been described 'as a regional system of branches, based on ties of caste and kinship, to which children were sent for their apprenticeship. If their first profits were deemed sufficient, they were taken on as partners or could set up their own agency.'[22]

Why European and not Eurasian?

That use of family in trade and commerce was not confined to India and the east more generally. A contemplation of the number of family firms in the early stages of industrialization in Europe reinforces the view that, from the economic standpoint, the single individual (even the conjugal family), not to speak of the lonely Robinson Crusoe aided by his black servant, does not provide the main model for the development of the firm. Employees, on the other hand, are more likely to be 'individualists' than are employers, but then this has generally been true of the poor, especially the landless labourers. Traditionally in China, as in India, it was the rich who lived in joint families, the poor in 'stem'. *The Forsyte Saga, Dallas, Dynasty*, these are all histories of entrepreneurship among rich family firms.

'Familism' in its various forms is no bar to industrialization. Indeed the firm may try to imitate the family. One of the interesting aspects of Japanese industrialization is the deliberate encouragement in the firm of family ideals, with the managers attempting to inculcate a quasi-filial respect among their employees. In many societies there are organizations in which relationships of equality and inequality are expressed in kinship terms. Like God, the chief is father (or grandfather) of his people; members of trade unions are brothers as well as comrades. It would be difficult to assert that in all these cases kinship served to disguise the 'real' nature of the relationship. But it is undoubtedly the case that many managers would like to see their organizations run as 'one happy family' rather than divided by conflicts over wages and conditions of work. And in Japan the ideas of life-long employment, of patronal paternalism, of 'live and prosper together', were encouraged by management specifically to counter the influence of Marxist syndicalism, as well as to promote industrial growth. They were strikingly successful in both endeavours.

From the wider standpoint of the economy – and it is economic developments with which the argument is ultimately concerned – China was in a roughly similar situation to India (not only with regard to the importance of family enterprise). In the late Middle Ages, parts of that vast country

17

were more advanced from a proto-industrial standpoint than Europe. When Marco Polo visited the southern capital in the thirteenth century, he found Hangchow the greatest city in the world, one whose economy and social life surpassed anything in Europe at that time. These developments were not held back either by the kinship system, or by the 'Asiatic' society, nor yet by the absence of an appropriate economic ethic. The 'masses of the Chinese people were basically well fed, well clothed, and well housed throughout most of their history . . . (they ate well enough and had enough of a sense of security about survival to think beyond that primary problem)'.[23] Part of the reason lay in the fact that Chinese peasants were relatively lightly taxed by their government, presumably because 'defence' expenditure was limited (unlike in fragmented Europe), as was the amount required for the support of other 'great organizations' such as the religious ones. There was no 'tithe'; gifts to the gods were more voluntary.

Textile production was extensive, mainly rural, employing both domestic and wage-labour. Merchants strove for the profit and the loss. In many respects peasants in rural communities acted along lines not greatly dissimilar to those in other areas of Asia and Europe. In making this claim I am not trying to introduce a Euro-centred view into China, but rather arguing for the reverse, for the necessity of looking at developments in Europe from a wider perspective, of taking a different point of departure. Far from being marked by the stagnating features associated with Asiatic production, a centralized regime imposed the minimum of restrictions on its inhabitants, leaving freedom of choice in competitive market situations:

> During nearly two thousand years, an individual could sell his labour on the free market or sell himself, or a member of his family, on the slave-market. A slave could end his servitude by buying himself out. A person could obtain land by purchase or other means, renting it out or working it himself. Those who had capital could invest it in a variety of ways.[24]

Why European and not Eurasian?

Peasants engaged in non-agricultural work, including work for the market; workshops and factories existed, before the fifteenth century often organized by the state. The Office of Weaving and Dyeing had twenty-five large works producing different kinds of silk cloth. During the Tang (616–907) and Song (960–1279) dynasties, the government recruited workers on the free market; while some industries, especially those involved in the production of arms, were in the hands of the state, others such as mining and iron working were often private. In other areas, public and private industry produced similar objects, with the former material gradually giving way to the latter, especially after the fifteenth century, when that became capable of supplying sufficient goods.[25]

The textile industry in China, was a secondary seasonal activity for more than 2,000 years, stimulated not only by local needs but also by the fact that, for the greater part of its history, the government demanded taxes in kind, in the form of textiles, which it could then export. Until the twelfth century, these were of silk or 'grass cloth' since cotton was not available. But silk of better quality was also produced by artisans and factories in the town. This was exported to Europe, and eventually manufactured there, until it was taken over by the production of cotton which came from India. So too did the early mechanization, for example in the case of water-driven reeling machines, first established in Lucca, then Bologna and north Italy, later being surreptitiously taken to Britain to be incorporated into the early Industrial Revolution. So that, for many centuries, we should be thinking in continental terms, of a Eurasian rather than a European movement.

3

Domestic aspects of the 'miracle'

The family and kinship have played a great part in discussions of the European miracle. The growth of capitalism has been seen, for example by the American sociologist Talcott Parsons, as linked to the 'small family' in contrast to that of other societies, an instance of the 'capitalist' shift to individualism against earlier 'collectivism'. This thesis was energetically taken up by historical demographers, especially those associated with the pioneering work of Laslett and the Cambridge Group, who placed much emphasis on the existence of the line drawn by the statistician John Hajnal, which excluded much of southern Europe from the 'European marriage pattern' which they saw as favouring the growth of capitalism, especially in the countries of the Atlantic fringe.

I have earlier discussed various aspects of this thesis[1] but here I want to concentrate on two. The attenuation of kinship and the rise of individualism are two interconnected topics that have been central to westerners' understanding (both scholarly and folk) of the processes that have led to modernization in Europe and to its supposed retardation in the east. They have been especially prominent in discussions by demographers since at least the writings of Malthus[2] at the end of the eighteenth century. He is a key figure for scholarship in this domain and we shall return to him later;

20

following his distinction between different modes of population control in the east and west, many have seen them as related to the nature of the demographic transition in the Occident. But these factors have also been central to the broad approach adopted by historians, social theorists and related scholars, being linked to notions of rationality (at least 'western rationality'), to economic maximization and to entrepreneurship. Since they are so central in many explanatory schemes, they need to be looked at with particular care as some of these usages seem to have been misleading for the field of population studies.

If we consider the broad sweep of history since 1000 CE, there has undoubtedly been a lateral attenuation of kinship ties, in that wider networks and larger groups of kin, of persons recognized as related by blood and marriage, have become of less significance. What effect has the diminution of kinship ties had on 'population'? In other words, does the existence of large kinship groups or ranges of kin (and their character) affect decisions about the number or sex of children?

Kingroups

Let us look first at large kinship groups under the heading of clans or lineages, either patrilineal (as with the Roman *gens*) or matrilineal (as with the Asante *abusua* of west Africa), and, on the other hand, various forms of bilateral kindred as in Anglo-Saxon England. First, it has been claimed that such kingroups (lineages) desire to extend their power base and therefore want to increase their numbers. That is a theoretical possibility, although quite what form this encouragement would take is difficult to see, unless at the level of an ideology (or concern) being instilled in particular members of the group and internalized by them. Decisions about reproduction necessarily involve an individual or couple, concerned at some point with resources, although some promptings may come from close kin or affines. But even in lineage societies such pressures emerge in the context of the small group, the lineal 'family', which until the last hundred years will have been just as implicated as in earlier societies.

Wider kingroups often use a 'classificatory' terminology, which appears to imply collective identities. For example, the wives of one's father's brothers may be termed 'mother', as indeed may all the wives of members of the lineage or clan of the same generation; equally one's brothers' wives are one's wives. In the nineteenth century, some scholars assumed this meant collective sexual or mothering arrangements, but field research casts doubts on whether that was ever the case. Sexual access was sometimes allowed, under special circumstances, to the wife of a twin brother among the LoDagaa of northern Ghana, but that was essentially comparable to the practice of a man sleeping with the son's wife, known as *chokhatch* amongst the Slavs. Sexual rights were otherwise particularized; so too with mothering. A mother's co-wife (a 'mother') might breastfeed a child when asked, or might look after the child on a longer-term basis if the mother was seriously ill, or indeed had died. But, although a number of women would be known as 'mother' (or as 'wife'), the particular mother that had borne you was always given special recognition; at this level, there was rarely any confusion of identities.

It seems doubtful if the character of kinship groups – that is, whether they are patrilineal, matrilineal or bilateral – has much affect on population variables. In the survey carried out in Ghana by Goody and Addo,[3] there was no effective difference in the numbers of children relative to membership of different groups. Respondents to our questions seemed to be aiming at maximum fertility, recognizing the restriction on birth-spacing as a consequence of the post-partum taboo on intercourse; indeed this taboo seems to have been seen as a means of maximizing rather than of restricting fertility under conditions of breastfeeding. But mortality was high, particularly among infants, so that, while Africa had seen the emergence of the first *Homo sapiens*, its rate of population increase over the last millennium – and over previous millennia – had been very gradual (until the twentieth century), giving rise to relatively low population densities compared with other continents that had been inhabited for a shorter time-span but had adopted different socio-economic courses. In most cases, pressures to reproduce will be balanced by a concern about the resources needed to establish a distinct family, resulting in the elaboration of specific 'strategies of heirship'. In China, until the advent of the Second World War, poorer families would have fewer children than richer ones since they had fewer resources to share between them. However, those without any resources at all may have had no such constraints.[4]

The existence of these strategies of heirship, which in Eurasia preferred direct lineal to lateral transmission when a person died, meant that there was already a degree of individualization, a form of attenuation of kinship. Children were given preference as heirs over more distant kin; indeed daughters took precedence over the male children of close lateral kin, separating off this small unit as a focus of inheritance. Lateral kin were then excluded. But that did not mean that a large pool of direct offspring was to be welcomed, since, before the days of individual wage-earning, access to the property required to gain a livelihood was obviously restricted; the greater the number of *surviving* children, the smaller the share for each, with the possibility of them dropping down in the social scale if unable to maintain their expected standard of living. The alternative to such 'misery' lay in restricting the number of births, taking care to have sufficient resources to provide for surviving children, after infant and adolescent mortality had taken their toll. That degree of calculation (though different individuals might make different choices) was already present in the major post-Bronze Age societies of Europe and Asia before the millennium commenced.

That is to say, there was and is, even in pre-modern societies, some calculation of the pros and cons of increasing the number of offspring, and this strategy of heirship (and of management) was carried out not at the lineage, clan or

The Eurasian Miracle

kinship level, but at that of the domestic group or household, as the Russian scholar Chayanov observed in a much-discussed work.[5] In other words, in peasant societies the strategies of reproduction were basically affairs not for wider kingroups but for the low-level productive units, just as they are in the present day. It is true that, in peasant households, some wider kinship concerns will make themselves felt, since close kin may also be closer spatially and economically, in terms of having interests in the same plot of land or in sharing tools and, occasionally, the same pool of labour. While these units were (and still are) slightly larger than those of many urban communities, what has really made the difference to individual calculations has been the shift to paid employment for the vast majority of people. Each individual is employed as a unit, not (in general) because of family or lineage. And both the husband and the wife and eventually their children are all separately (individually) employed.

This was not formerly the case, when education was aimed at reproducing religious or other communities, not at pointing towards future employment, which rather took place in training at the home. Even today there is some continuity, even joint enterprise, with the family, especially in the catering trade (but more in France than in Britain), and family business remains highly significant, even in more capitalist countries such as the United States.[6] But in most cases each person has his or her own pay packet and is responsible for paying their own taxes or receiving their own benefits; each individual has his or her own personal relationship with the state and its agencies.

It is at this level that decisions concerning procreation were made, rarely at the societal or intermediary level, though more general pressures there may militate in favour of pro-natalist or other family policies, for example by arranging taxation benefits for married couples, through children's allowances or by support for single parents. But overall these policies have made surprisingly little difference, with the notable exception of the one-child policy in China, which by and large was pushing in an accepted or acceptable direction.

Domestic aspects of the 'miracle'

There has been much discussion of the difference between pro-natalist regimes and others (stressing individual choice) but with few exceptions the effects on population trends seem to have been small. For example, the differences in family structure between regimes pursuing collectivist (socialist) or individualist (capitalist) policies are much less marked than many theories would project. Nor has there been a great divergence between Europe (or the west), seen as following the latter policy, and Asia (or the east) viewed as more attached to the former course.

Kinship

However, although wider groups virtually disappear, it is not clear that there has been any attenuation in the ties that bind smaller groups, families; indeed, quite the contrary is often asserted by those historians who posit the growth in modern times of the affective family, of conjugal ties and even of parenthood and the household. The evidence for making such an assessment is difficult to handle; while wider ties have contracted, narrower ones may have in certain ways been reinforced, even though in most cases they no longer serve as the basic relations of production as they once did, and still do in most agricultural communities. The absence of that link tends to release the individual couple from having to take wider family pressures into account in making decisions about marriage, divorce and procreation. There may be a limited pressure in maintaining a distinction between marriage and other sexual unions (concubinage in some terminologies, but the word places the onus of illegitimacy on the woman), that is, in formalizing a union. On the other hand, it is not clear if, for procreation, such pressures were ever very important. Parents and grandparents might express their wishes for progeny, and thus reinforce natalist propensities. Indeed, that may still be a minor factor in decision-making. But it is doubtful if more distant kin were ever very significant in this context.

The Eurasian Miracle

Regarding Europe and Asia, the similarities in family structure, and to that extent of population trends, seem to have been many,[7] despite the claims of Malthus and the many other east–west binarists who have followed the same general line. Demographers have tended to emphasize differences rather than similarities and thus to neglect the convergences. These I will discuss later when considering individualism. One interesting test case is to look at the difference between socialist and capitalist regimes, both between and within east and west, an issue we return to in considering Malthus on China. Once again the overall differences in population trends in relation to kinship have not in the end been all that striking, despite ideological predilictions for collectivism in the first instance and for individualism in the second. But collective production units such as farms, communes or cooperatives have not encouraged wider kinship ties; quite the opposite. The unit of production has been the focus of collective ties; within it, the tendency outside ownership is for the members to be treated more or less on an individual basis. One of the main functions of the family in other regimes, not only capitalist, has been the transmission of property, material and immaterial ('symbolic capital'), over the generations. Socialist programmes have specifically set themselves the task of modifying such inherited inequalities between individuals and families, and in Communist states of abolishing them altogether, not only in relation to the means of production – which in any case were no longer under the family's immediate control. However, this programme ran counter to trends within the unit of reproduction, which may have even been a contributory factor in the downfall of these regimes, through lowering targets for the accumulation of goods by inhibiting their intra-familial transfer.

As a consequence, notions of collectivization at the level of the economy have not been paralleled by an emphasis on the larger family or the larger kinship group, in the shape of either the extended family or the clan. Ideologically, many socialists looked back towards a supposedly earlier state of affairs when property was held in common by large kinship groups – primitive Communism as sketched out by the American lawyer L. H. Morgan, and taken up from his *Ancient Society* by Marx and Engels. As far as the family was concerned, even rights in women were said to be owned in common in the past, like land. For the distant past, we know that both these claims were imaginary. Kingroups were certainly larger in most pre-industrial societies but at their core were always to be found relatively small households or 'families' which were the significant unit of production, but more definitely of reproduction. There is little evidence that larger households (the so-called 'extended family') went along with these wider kingroups, except to the extent that, in relatively stable agricultural communities, larger numbers of relatives inevitably gather in one vicinity, occasionally in the same house. What disappeared in the course of time were large kingroups, many of their functions being taken over by the state or by the church.

Individualism

The other major topic, strongly associated with the first, is the rise of individualism. Individualism (basically seen as a masculine attribute) has been appropriated by the west as a concept purporting to explain entrepreneurship and modernization in western Europe and America, where it is a typical quality of the male adventurer who goes to live on the expanding frontier. The argument has been taken up by many historians and sociologists in relation to the emergence of this quality in Europe at the time of the Reformation. The thesis bears the stamp of intellectuals like the nineteenth-century sociologists Spencer and Durkheim, but it also strikes a chord in popular conceptions of the past. In their books on Tudor England, both the historians Thomas and Macfarlane saw the emergence of economic individualism in the sixteenth century as linked to the attitudes towards magic and witchcraft.[8] The problem with the argument is not so much that it is altogether wrong – we are rightly convinced that important changes took place at this time – but that the concept is inadequate to deal with those changes. Macfarlane's resolution of the problem is to seek the origins of individualism in an earlier England. 'Individualism' has been discovered at earlier periods, not only in England but in western Europe as a whole. Part of the concern of the historian of religion John Bossy lies in his view that the sacramental theory of marriage held by the Catholic church carried 'individualistic implications' which had been stressed by canon lawyers since about 1300.[9] The historian Sheehan[10] also insists upon the individualistic implications of the consensual theory of marriage adopted by Alexander III and Innocent III, and developed by canonists and theologians from the twelfth through the fourteenth centuries. Individualism was not, therefore, an invention of the Reformation. Nevertheless, it was seen by Weber as being encouraged by Calvinistic Protestantism. This branch of Protestantism was characterized by a religious individualism stemming from the conviction that a believer did not require spiritual intermediaries with God (as in Catholicism), and therefore such persons possessed a mental landscape marked by an emphasis on self-reliance and on self-direction. Their reliance on conscience, Weber thought, encouraged risk-taking individuals.

The association of individualism with later Europe and America has been assumed by many, indeed most, western historians. But individualism, at best, is very difficult to define for analytic purposes and its role differs in different contexts. It has politico-legal, economic, familial and even religious facets. The political aspect is associated with the notion of democracy in opposition to Oriental despotism, empires and authoritarianism; in time, it goes back to the city states of ancient Greece (although they had their occasional tyrants and perpetual slaves). Allowing people to vote or to be consulted in other ways could be considered more individualistic. It permitted individuals to express their personal opinions and not simply accept authoritarian forms of government. But consultation existed elsewhere, democracy did not flourish in Europe alone, and there not until at least the eighteenth century. No tradition of political democracy was permanently established there following antiquity, except in the minds and writings of later European scholars (and perhaps among pirates, rebels and similar marginal groups). Of course, people's opinions were taken into account, but so they had to be in most regimes.

Economic 'individualism', entrepreneurship, is a feature of merchants everywhere, not simply a western inheritance epitomized in Robinson Crusoe; it characterized the search for metals following the Bronze Age, the exchange of goods with outsiders and many other transactions carried out on a worldwide basis. Individualism, especially when applied to Europe, is often associated with 'rationality' and the capacity to work out the best plan of action (which it is thought the collectivity may distort). Along with a capacity for innovation and exploration, they are claimed by European scholars as attributes of their own societies in an attempt to explain the origins of 'capitalism' in the west. But rationality is just as difficult to define across the board as individuality, and in any case is again found in some contexts in all societies, as is individualism.

In respect of the family, the notion of individualism is tied up with that of the nuclear or small households in contrast to 'extended families' or even clans and lineages. It is linked to the supposedly unique western family and originated, according to some, with the ancient Indo-Europeans. It is associated by Mann and others with rain-fed farming (rather than with irrigation), with forests and dispersed settlement, to long-standing geographical factors which led in their turn to the elaboration of private property and of capitalism.

These arguments concerning the relationship of family, individualism and rationality to development, in the demographic as in the economic sphere, have been raised in the Great Debate, pursued by many European historians, social scientists and demographers, followed even by some in Asia when they have been concerned with the problem of why the west achieved modernization, capitalism, industrialization, and the east did not (at least, not at the same time). The

29

demographic aspects of this concern and its implication for the history of the family are often phrased in Malthusian terms, especially in the contrast between Europe and China. Of course, the idea that Europe was more individualistic in its outlook was not confined to Malthus and the demographers. As we have remarked, in America it was associated with 'the frontier' (as if only there did the boundary beckon). On a wider historical level, it was early found in 'democratic' Greece and its successors, as distinct from the 'despotic' or arbitrary Orient, or in ecological terms in the rain-fed peasant agriculture of the west as against the irrigated control demanded by the arid east. Western systems were later linked to decentralized feudalism in which seigneurial property was moving towards full private property, in contrast to which, in the view of Weber and many others, in the east the monarch kept ownership in his own hands.

That is the argument pursued by Mann in his book *The Sources of Social Power*,[11] which traces European individualism back to the Iron Age European peasant. These Indo-Europeans had learnt from the civilizations of the Near East and the classical world, but were not held back by the same constraints. Individualism is also associated, as by the anthropologist Louis Dumont, with Christianity; that religion, he claims (following Weber), promoted 'ethical individual conduct'. In his opinion, these factors made Europe particularly favourable to the advent of capitalism. That same theme is also central to the more ecological argument of Eric Jones, author of *The European Miracle*,[12] that the extensive agriculture of early Europe, with dispersed holdings (and nuclear families), produced 'the cellular, high-energy, high-consumption life-style and *individualist* performances of the Celtic and Germanic tribes'.[13] As a result, Europeans alone know how to conserve the gifts of their environment and not waste them 'in a mere insensate multiplication of the common life', like Malthus' Chinese.[14] That capacity developed with their practice not of irrigation but of a simpler type of farming.

Such ideas about development have been heavily criticized in recent years by some non-European scholars who have

uncovered 'sprouts of capitalism', and therefore of individualism and enterprise, in their own societies; but their influence on demographic and family studies in Europe has been
slow to take effect. In the European context, one of the most
trenchant critics has been the American geographer J. M.
Blaut, who argues that the notion that individualism, especially with regard to property rights, owed its conception
to Rome or to ancient Germany, and that such ideas were
absent in non-European cultures, was mistaken but consis-
tent with colonialists' claim that such conquered people had
no property rights (the colonial myth of emptiness) and so
their lands could have western property law imposed upon
them, making way for modernization, for alienation, for
development.[15]

Even Marx took up the notion, which he sees as related
to that of Oriental despotism (marked by the absence of
freedom which accompanied westernization). The idea was
also central to the work of Weber. That thesis has been
recently criticized by a Japanese historian of the samurai who
comments that, in the later (Tokagawa) period,

> the presence of a clear sense of resilient individuality emerged
> in expressions of self-assertiveness combined with dignity and
> pride. A sense of individuality is deeply connected to capaci-
> ties for courage and deliberation, which are necessary to initi-
> ate change. . . . This kind of intense sense of selfhood could,
> when properly connected to an appropriate social goal, serve
> to generate an initiative for social change.[16]

Comparing Weber's analysis of the Protestant ethic with her
own study of samurai culture, Ikegami concludes that 'out
of a completely different cultural matrix the Japanese samurai
also constructed a society that was conducive to self-control
and concentration on long-term ends, as well as an individualistic attitude that encourages risk-taking'.[17] Europe again
had no monopoly.

Such an association of individualism with the east chal-
lenges western views of the uniqueness of their cultures,

which often see conformity as the dominant characteristic of eastern societies. It is generally true that people see conformity to norms as being marks of the 'other', whereas we are ourselves governed by individualistic, rational criteria. The author of this study, Ikegami, on the other hand, insists that in Japanese history a counter-culture 'supports individualistic expressions and actions';[18] what she calls 'honorific individualism' is frequently encountered in individuals 'who dare to take initiatives for change while taking significant social and personal risks'. This 'honorific individualism' emerges 'as a form of "possessive individualism", a conviction about the self that grew up among landed elites, who required a firm sense of self-possession paralleling their pride in the ownership of land',[19] thus recalling the association of seventeenth-century political philosophies of individualism with property ownership; the mode of property possession was linked to the mode of understanding selfhood.

Malthus and the east

If this was so, then, just as Ikegami has detached the notion of individualism from the western context, extending it to other landed elites, so it becomes necessary to extend it yet further to other forms of 'property possession', which were not necessarily associated with 'capitalism' or with 'feudalism'. For many observers of 'other cultures' have commented upon the individualism of the people they have studied. The anthropologist Evans-Pritchard remarked upon this feature among the Nuer of the southern Sudan and he has been followed by countless others. Clearly, we are not dealing with societies undergoing the same rapidity of change as in the European or, later, Japanese cases, but individual members of such societies are always having to adjust to some change (especially religious change, but also with the regular problems of the developmental cycle of domestic groups), and so they are never members of entirely static societies.[20]

Domestic aspects of the 'miracle'

Malthus, the founding father of modern demography, is much implicated in these arguments. For him, the existence of preventative checks on population growth, such as he found in modern Europe, was tied to the notion of moral restraint, whereas in other societies positive (external) checks on such developments operated through a mixture of misery and vice; the latter were largely involuntary, whereas moral restraint was purely volitional, an aspect of rational decision-making, operating on the basis of individual choice. Europe had the latter but China, only the former.

In their important study on China, two demographers, Lee and Feng, refute the Malthusian paradigm for the east, including the binary division between positive and preventative checks, where the latter are based upon later marriage age and upon a moral restraint only available in the west. True, Europeans married later but, when they did so, they had more children than those in the east, who were more 'restrained'. That deals with the Weberian and Malthusian arguments. However, they continue in a binary mode to characterize Asia as exhibiting collective control, Europe as exhibiting an individualistic one. Apart from the one-child policy recently applied by the state, the evidence they provide seems to run against such a dichotomy. For example, Chinese marriage forms are rightly described as variable, varying by gender, by class, by birth order and by individual circumstance; such a variety required individual choice to select the most appropriate strategy. That is also the case with the decision, not so infrequent, to kill a child (usually female). These are not collective decisions but very much individual, or couple-determined, choices. The same too with marriage; 'although not all Chinese plan their fertility or control the survivorship of their children, all do plan the marriage of their own children'.[21] They have to 'plan' the marriage since that is the point at which major property transactions and residential shifts take place, but this is done on a largely individual basis. If the married couple are not content with what is proposed, they may, as Wolf and Huang[22] have importantly pointed out, and as recognized by Lee and Feng,[23] resort to 'wrecking' tactics, which means a low fertility and more frequent break-down.

'Family planning', write Lee and Feng, 'is associated with our increased ability to decide deliberately . . . to control reproduction', and is linked to 'a new sense of control over ourselves and the natural world'.[24] The rise of such consciousness appears to be connected in their minds to 'the spread of *individual* decision making associated with the rise of small families, the increase in literacy, the emergence and diffusion of Western *individualism*, and the growing penetration of market economies'.[25] Rightly seeing Europe as the cradle of the last phase of 'modernization', some scholars perceive a European origin for the demographic transition from high to low mortality and fertility, and consider that 'the European roots of individualism and even the European development of nineteenth-century capitalism are intertwined and embedded in a European family and demographic structure that encouraged such revolutionary social and economic changes'.[26] But family planning itself is no monopoly of Europe. As Lee and Feng remark of China, 'planning demographic events has always been an important part of life'.[27] Contrary to Malthus' opinion, and that of the many western demographers who have followed him, the east was not limited to the 'positive' checks such as famine. Family planning did go on, which indeed permitted the demographic transition eventually to take place more rapidly even than in the west, and to take place on a household level, even though this continued to occur in the context of more collective considerations. While in the past the Chinese had controlled fertility (for marital fertility was no higher than in the west) and killed their (mainly female) children 'in response to the dictates of household economy, today they reduce their fertility largely in response to the perceived needs and strong dictates of the national economy [the one-child policy], and increasingly to *maximize their family welfare*'.[28]

However, the authors continue to see a broad difference from the west, in that 'In China demographic decisions are never individual'.[29] The collective needs of family and state have to be taken into account. Marriage is 'not a personal arrangement' but a family one. Lee and Feng insist that in China 'deliberate fertility control has long been within the calculus of conscious choice',[30] yet without pursuing the case for a collective consciousness they argue that the current tradition is the result of 'new collective institutions and collective goals, not of new ideas' – in contrast to the western situation which involved a revolutionary extension of individual decision from marriage to fertility. But all this conscious planning is seen as firstly traditional (in other words, China was marked by the early recognition of such checks), and secondly as involving the family (or the community or the state), and was never, they claim, an individual prerogative as in western individualism. Yet previously the authors have, rightly in my view, proclaimed that 'the Chinese demographic system was characterized by a multiplicity of choices that *balanced romance with arranged marriage*, marital passion with marital restraint, and parental love with the decision to kill or give away children'.[31] But they see this human agency as exercised at the collective rather than the individual level, although I would query whether we can discern an effective difference here. It is true that the recent one-child policy has been organized by the state, and this constitutes their prime example, but how different is this from Rajiv Gandhi's attempts in India, or from French or German pro-natalism in Europe? Strategies of heirship of the kind embodied in the decision to adopt or to kill (both of them basically individual or possibly conjugal) are not made on the level of the lineage or collective but by individuals. The application of the distinction between collective and individual to a cultural level seems to be very much part of the same binary division that Malthus made about population restraints; it is a theme I have pursued elsewhere in the context of the features claimed to contrast the east and the west.[32] Individual choices related to property were included in both eastern and western decision-making. Each maximized their opportunities 'within an opportunity structure defined to a large degree by collective institutions, interests and ideologies';[33] these differed (with lineages in the case of the Chinese) but nevertheless, in both cases, human agency operated basically through individual actors.

Certainly, any individual or couple in China might have to take into account the opinions of other close family members, but the final decisions are taken by individuals or couples, not by collectivities. The authors refer to 'the close supervision of the collective family'[34] but no evidence of any effect on such decision-making is provided, and this contention is perhaps as much a 'myth' as the Malthusian ones. It was Chinese couples (and individuals) who in the end controlled the 'passion between the sexes'. While the pressures may be different from those in the west, to characterize the European as individualistic and the Asian as collective seems to fall into the same mistaken semantic and conceptual binarism as countless European observers. Is this not a case, as the authors point out with regard to Malthus, of easterners taking on western myths about their own behaviour? Is it not parallel to the characterization of one variety of a high-pressure regime (high fertility, high mortality) as the 'Chinese structure' which Lee and Feng take care to refute?[35]

More generally, the politico-economic system in China, with its 'collective' families, is contrasted with Europe's 'long tradition of individualism'. It is the case that, in China, the unilineal clans and lineages that we have encountered earlier played an important part in social life, whereas in the west kinship groupings were organized bilaterally (as in the Anglo-Saxon feuds), and in any case these extended groupings (or ranges of kin) were whittled down under pressure from the church and the state.[36] But was the contrast so clear at the level of demographic decision-making? The 'collective family mentality', Lee and Feng assert, leads to most adoption in China being within the lineage.[37] But it could well be argued that for a man to adopt his brother's son in order to make him an heir or a 'family member' was the opposite of a collective mentality – rather, an individualistic approach to heirship. No one, as the authors say, should go childless, and that is calculated on a *purely* individual (or couple) basis, not on a collective one. The adoptive parents (or parent) were maximizing not 'collective utility' but individual advantage. For example, 'the response to economic conditions could vary greatly from individual to individual'.[38] So the authors conclude, contrary to one of Malthus' and their own major contentions, that 'despite its size and its collective nature, [the Chinese system] was able to regulate population growth, through first family and later state control'.[39] They contrast family control with Europe's 'long tradition of individualism'. But, in fact, whatever the ideological position, demographic decisions in Europe often took into account close 'familial' concerns, at least until the Industrial Revolution, and even subsequently they were mostly made in the context of dyadic (couple, family) relationships, even though in the twentieth century individual wage-packets, state provision and family circumstance might permit some parents 'to go it alone'. In earlier times the contrast seems less obvious, except in terms of the existence of wider clan (unilineal) groups which seem to have left such decision-making to the smallest familial (kin) groups. The authors claim that 'the extended family and the household, not the individual or the individual couple, was the basic decision-making body'.[40] But most households consisted of the latter and, for wider involvement, they offer no proof as far as demographic behaviour is concerned. Indeed the contention contradicts some of the other suggestions about individual or couple-based 'strategies of heirship' based upon 'individual' holdings.

In the 1960s, population growth in China underwent an unprecedented explosion which the authors attribute to the collapse of the traditional unit of population control with a reduction in mortality and the resort to unconstrained high fertility. They see family authority:

> as deteriorating after the 1911 Revolution. Parents no longer had a legal claim over children's property, arranged marriages were outlawed, and we might also add there were pressures against marriage transfers and in favour of 'love marriages'. With the advent of socialism these tendencies were enhanced

but at the same time, in collective work units compensation for participation was awarded mainly on an individual not a family basis.[41]

With the coming of the Communes, collectives into which people were shepherded, in 1958, individuals no longer had to plan their holding of children as before. In this way, the socialization of the means of production meant that individual responsibility was abandoned. The more children you had, the greater the claim on collective resources. I have heard the same rationale for unlimited reproduction in Nkrumah's Ghana, when a friend explained how he had no qualms about having more children, since the state would educate them to help themselves. Similar views were expressed in England in the 1950s. Under these conditions, fertility control had to be applied at a collective level. But that did not imply a shift of ideology from the individualist to the collective (at the demographic level); both elements were relevant. It rather represented the continuation of the same policies as before, but these were now freed from resource constraint by social factors – that is, until the state stepped in.

Collective efforts towards fertility control made by the Chinese authorities in the mid twentieth century were certainly highly successful and strongly supported, but the authors comment that there was 'some individual family resistance'.[42] That qualification seems to contradict the supposed dominance of the collective and absence of western individualism that is thought to have enabled Europe to control its population through rational calculation. Indeed, they emphasize that Chinese parents did have methods of adjusting the population that were not collective in this sense, and they 'produced and kept children only when it was to their advantage.'[43] That seems to reinforce the degree of convergence in decision-making. Otherwise why do the same conclusions concerning collectivism not apply to the Chinese in Taiwan, Hong Kong, Singapore? Why is the same not true of the collectivist Soviet Union and of post-1989 Russia? The binary division, however, pushes in another direction.

Again, 'Whereas individualistic society required the rule of law to protect human rights, collective society requires the rule of autocracy to enforce collective goals'.[44] That seems an unsound generalization to which the authors have been led by their overly binary approach to 'comparative social structure and social behaviour'. If Malthus was wrong about adopting a binary approach to demographic checks, he was right, they claim, about 'the different social and political orientations of each society [east and west]'.[45] That assertion seems to be open to much disagreement, especially as the overarching 'collectivist' ideology of the Chinese government comes direct from western Marxist sources, and may indeed be regarded as part of the spread of western (modernizing) ideas.

In their final chapter, the authors seek to modify their binary contrast, at the same time as qualifying the views of the population scholars Macfarlane and Todd about the relation between demography (and the family) and the political economy.[46] Contrary to the general hypothesis, they (rightly) see collective elements in western political thought (for example Marx!), and individualistic ones in Confucianism. For example, half the officials in the late imperial period were appointed by competitive examination, a rate of mobility higher than in Tudor or Stuart England. On the family level, the Qin dynasty assessed a multiple household tax on those with more than one residential unit, even when these were composed of sons and brothers: 'Within two years, customs had changed to the point that "when a son reached adulthood [and married], he set up his own household with a share of the property, . . . if he lent his father a rake or hoe, he behaved as if he acted magnanimously"'.[47] So the collective features of the family, even filial piety, had a measure of flexibility. Lee and Feng recognize that the binary contrast can be over-drawn,[48] and that contemporary approaches, especially the analysis of data, militate against such large-scale contrasts. They warn that this trend makes the world less understandable. True, but there is no alternative in the social sciences to the recognition of complexity where this exists, even if this means querying the value of the time-honoured opposition between individualistic and collectivist behaviour, with which the west has long attempted to set apart the ancient (or earlier), the Oriental and the primitive from the modern (and not so modern) west.[49]

This chapter has tried to follow up the work of Asian scholars, especially Lee and Feng, and Ikegami, as well as nationalist historians who have rejected the idea that, in the movement to modernization, the comparative advantages, familial, economic, entrepreneurial, religious, always lay with the west. In particular, it has criticized the influential notions of Malthus, Marx and Weber, some of which have had a negative influence on population studies, especially in relation to individualism and the role of the 'extended' family. Both in demography and in the social sciences generally, these notions have tended to 'primitivize' non-European cultures. In the west, this amended view is certainly a minority one, though gaining increasing support; in the east, it is bolstered by much recent research and theoretical thinking. I have pursued three kinds of comparison which overlap at various points: the first involves time, earlier and later ('modern'); the second involves space, the east and the west; and the third, socialist and capitalist regimes; individualism has been constantly seen as a characteristic of the second elements, collectivism of the first. At the level of the family, kin ties remain important in modern societies and are often intrinsic to capitalist industrial and commercial enterprise, even though wider ties, rarely of great significance for reproduction, have been whittled away. As for individualism, its 'rise' is very problematic, given its importance in earlier periods and its questionable status in many spheres of an industrial society, which is emphatically collectively organized in terms of work and education.

4

Eurasia and the Bronze Age

I have so far been concerned to criticize the notion of the
European miracle. But I now want to turn to discuss the
Eurasian miracle and later to outline the temporary advantage that the west, Europe, gained in the nineteenth and
twentieth centuries within that wider framework. I see this
advantage as real within a wider context in which one found,
and continues to find in a more modified way, the phenomenon of alternation in societies that benefited from the Bronze
Age. It was that age that brought together east and west in
a single set of achievements. The concept of the Urban Revolution of the Bronze Age is associated with the name of the
prehistorian Gordon Childe, and was clearly connected with
the American lawyer L. H. Morgan's concept of civilization
and the culture of cities in *Ancient Society*,[1] and probably
with more general sources.[2] The notion of civilization has
been much confounded by sociologists such as the Anglo-
German Norbert Elias, who see the Civilizing Process as
beginning in early modern Europe; and even by the French
historian Fernand Braudel, who writes of civilizations
'confronting one another in the Mediterranean' when he
is referring to the meeting of Islam and Christianity.
    One great advantage of Childe's notion is precisely that it
does not privilege the west but describes a common historical

development that took place in the ancient Near East, reaching Egypt and the Aegean, India and China. Now the cultural affinity at this period between the main Eurasian urban civilizations runs up against the notion of a radical discontinuity or difference that is the basis of some of the major and most influential of socio-historical concepts about world development. According to the dominant European view in the nineteenth century, looking back from a standpoint of their undoubted achievements after the Renaissance and the Industrial Revolution, historians and sociologists (and to some extent anthropologists) felt they had to account for these differences. So the west was seen as passing through a number of stages of development from ancient society, to what have been called feudalism and capitalism. The east on the other hand was marked by what Marx saw as 'Asiatic exceptionalism', characterized by hydraulic agriculture and by despotic government (which was needed to organize it), whereas the west, especially Europe, was rain-fed and consultative. That is not just a Marxist argument; it was held in a different form by Weber and other historians, and we have come across versions of it put forward by the sociologist Mann, and by others who are wedded to a consideration of long-term European advantage – Eurocentric historians, the geographer Blaut calls them. And those versions take many forms – for example, as we have seen, in the highly influential account given by Malthus of the supposed failures of China to control her population because she did not have the internalized restraints of the west. This view bears some resemblances to Weber's idea of the role of the Protestant ethic in the birth of capitalism, widely taken up by the demographic-historians of the Cambridge Group under the inspirational leadership of Peter Laslett.

Certainly, there were broad differences in the sequencing of social life in the west and east. In the former, the fall of the classical empires meant a partial decay of urban civilization, the disappearance of some towns, and the increased importance of the countryside and its rulers, leading to what has been called 'feudalism'. In the European account of the process, this stage is seen as a 'progressive' move in terms of world history, leading eventually to the birth of a new kind of town, beginning with the communes of north Italy, sheltering their freedom-loving bourgeoisie, their autonomous governments, and the various features that made them the forerunners of capitalism and modernization. But it also goes back to earlier views of Asia as 'despotic' in contrast to 'democratic' Greece.

The notion of Asiatic exceptionalism has recently been under fire. It has been implicitly criticized by Eric Wolf in his work on *Europe and the Peoples without History*[3] where he suggests that the authority systems of both the east and the west, despotic or democratic, should be seen as variants of one another, types of the 'tributary state', with versions in the east being sometimes more centralized than those in the west. The implications for the later development of capitalism have been firmly criticized by a new generation of scholars who have rejected or modified the notion of European advantage before the Industrial Revolution, and whose work I have discussed in a recent book.[4] But little attempt has so far been made to link up these new perspectives on post-classical history with the earlier, archaeological, background and with the work of Gordon Childe. If there was a broad unity in terms of 'civilization' at the time of the Bronze Age, how did the 'exceptionalism' subsequently develop? Did it ever develop at all? Was the disappearance of towns (and the prevalence of 'feudalism') ever anything but a particular western European episode in world history? Because, around the Mediterranean, towns, especially ports, continued a vigorous life – in Constantinople, Damascus, Baghdad and Alexandria. In Europe, Venice soon recaptured the spirit and activity of its Roman past and vigorously entered into a profitable exchange with the east. And if we look at the more or less continuous history of towns in Asia we get a very different picture from the one gained by concentrating on the decay of urban culture and on the rural mode of production in western Europe. Elsewhere, towns and ports did not disappear, to be reborn as forerunners of capitalist enterprise; they continued to flourish throughout Asia and formed the nodes of exchange, manufacture, education and other specialist activity that pointed towards later developments. While the new towns of western Europe doubtless had some particular features, they were not unique in the way that Weber, Braudel[5] and others have posited. Towns were representative of early 'capitalist' activity wherever they were found, in India, in China, in the Near East. They were centres of specialist employment, of written culture, of commerce carried out by merchants and artisans of various degrees of complexity. Indeed, while advanced industrial capitalism was developed in the west, it is a travesty of world history to see its early growth as being unique to that continent. The usual criteria of advanced capitalism are industrialization and high finance or extensive commerce. With mass production in industrial conditions, finance had to play a greater role and exchange became more intense, but neither were new European features of the economy. Nor was industrialization. That process marked some of the early manufacturing activity of China, especially in the sphere of ceramics, but also in the production of paper. Within Europe, the industrial production of textiles certainly did not begin with the English cotton industry in the mid eighteenth century. It had already started in Italy in the fourteenth with the reeling of silk, which gave the country's industry a very considerable comparative advantage.[6] These processes were developed in competition with the silk imported from China and the Near East.

We need to query these old myths and take another look at the supposed discontinuity with the Bronze Age between ancient societies and feudalism. Elsewhere, the history of urbanization displays a very different profile. Urban cultures, with their 'luxury' element leading to its own contradictions (see chapter 6), continued to develop and change from those earlier times. The case of cooked food[7] and, indeed, of luxury products more generally, such as domesticated flowers,[8] helps us to understand this process. I have chosen these two manifestations of cultural 'differences' because they are largely absent from Africa and very much present in the societies of

Eurasia and the Bronze Age

Eurasia, not confined to Europe or to 'capitalism' but found in all the major post-Bronze Age ones. I use them again here as examples of the 'cultural' similarities between east and west, ones that are related to the economy but to aspects of culture (and knowledge) more generally. In the first instance, I felt that too simplistic comparisons were being made between the cookery of Africa and elsewhere. More account needed to be given to ethnological and archaeological realities, especially to class differences. From the standpoint of development, Africa was characterized by some strange anomalies. Iron had made its way across the Sahara and been widely adopted, using local laterite as low-grade ore to produce some expensive but indispensable metal by arduous methods: indispensable because used for instruments of war and for hunting and farming with the hoe. Restricted literacy too had reached Black Africa by way of Islam both in the western savannahs and along the eastern littoral. It was not widely used – mainly for religious purposes. In other respects, agriculturally for example, the continent was firmly placed in the Neolithic, not in the Bronze Age. If the wheel and the shaduf did cross the Sahara, neither were taken up. In pre-colonial times, animal traction did not exist. All cultivation was by means of the hoe (although with an iron blade) – even in some places with a digging stick. Under the conditions of soil and rainfall prevailing in the savannahs, this meant that, during the rainy season, a man could cultivate just about enough to feed his family (with their combined help) but leaving him with little surplus to employ any specialists (apart from smiths) or to pay for their produce, and too little to support an elaborate hierarchy of office holders. Chiefdoms and chiefs were, of course, to be found, some of considerable importance, but there was no real leisure class. Minor chiefs had to farm, as did trading and religious specialists. Under these conditions, there was some political stratification but little economic differentiation, certainly in terms of land. Everybody farmed what they needed to and, when the yield decreased, they moved on to a new part of the lineage (family) land which constituted a kind of reserve. Land was rarely a scarce good.

The Eurasian Miracle

With small differences in land holding and in economic status more generally, there was little tendency towards confining marriage to the same group. Economically, one union was more or less as good as any other. There were no economic 'classes' in this sense and few tendencies to marry in. Exogamy was preferred rather than endogamy because it created wider alliances. Under this regime, there was little difference in standards of living and little tendency for the emergence of different styles of life. There was virtually no differentiated cuisine (except sometimes in terms of the amount of meat and cereal available) and little likelihood of the emergence of subcultures.

I have described what I believe to be a typical chief's compound among the Gonja of northern Ghana. In this polygynous society, each wife had her own hut and each may well come from a different 'estate' in the society, one from a commoner group, another from the Muslims, traders and religious specialists, perhaps another from the chiefly estate, although this estate tended not to marry their 'sisters' who were considered 'too proud'. These women cooked on their own hearth of three stones set in the common open space of the courtyard round which their rooms had been built. Under these conditions, recipes tend to get shared; there was a homogenization of cooking, defeating any tendency for the evolution of different styles.

The major post-Bronze Age societies of Eurasia were very different. The plough immediately made it possible for one individual to farm a greater area than another, and it was therefore valuable to own more land. Land holding now became a fundamental criterion of difference, a basic feature of stratification. The big landowner commanded much greater economic resources than the smaller farmers. His family tended to be brought up differently and, therefore, to marry differently; the demand was for a 'match', depending upon the girl's 'portion' of the family's wealth. She needed to be cared for after marriage as she had been before, to eat as she had done in her natal household, which may have employed specialist cooks in their kitchen or purchased particular foods, such as the breads from those urban workers who baked them in their (Bronze Age) ovens. Under these conditions one finds the emergence of a differentiated cuisine, with different foods and recipes for the rich (prepared by their cooks, sometimes male) and for the poor (cooked by their wives). This basic form of cuisine represented the styles of life present in the various classes and crystallized the notion of a cultural hierarchy, based primarily on land holding or the ownership of the means of production. Frequently, the upper classes clustered together in towns rather than in their distant estates, among others of the same circles. This differentiated cuisine – cuisine as opposed to cooking – emerged in all the major post-Bronze Age states.

It all rested upon a complex, hierarchical division of labour, with one individual purchasing the labour power of another, as well as upon a more complex technology (such as ovens) and a wider set of socio-economic relationships (which permitted the import of spices). It also related very much to the communication (as well as the consumption) of recipes by means of the written word, especially when we are dealing with that special class of differentiated cuisines that is accepted as *haute cuisine*, like the Chinese, Indian, Arabic, Italian and French varieties.[9] These required not only the context of class in which to develop, but also a discriminating and leisured clientele capable of distinguishing the tastes, the smells and the appearance of the range of ingredients and of elaborating a set of 'understandings' (hardly 'rules') about the consumption of elite food. That happened in Beijing in China, for example, when literati from different provinces gathered and required restaurants to prepare elaborated versions of the dishes from their home areas, such as Szechwan and Canton. This elaboration demanded a discriminatory clientele of well-off eaters, who could command the best cooks, the best ingredients (often rare and expensive to find) and the best recipes.

To meet these requirements needed not necessarily a 'court society', in Elias' terms. It might also be generated by the bourgeoisie, by the town dwellers, the literati or administrators in China, as well as by the merchants whose documents for the Arab world have been examined by the French Arabist Rodinson. It is the town dwellers, the bourgeoisie, who have often provided the wider, richer, educated and elitest clientele that such a development requires.

Now what is interesting about the development of *hautes cuisines*, as with luxury culture more generally, is the fact that these have appeared in all the major civilizations in Eurasia, in what can be seen in very broad terms as roughly the same period. One can trace the emergence of a literature of connoisseurship in China, according to Clunas[10] and Brook,[11] in roughly the same epoch as its emergence in Europe. Similar statements could be made about developments in many of the arts, including the rejection of forms of figurative representation (icons) altogether (discussed in chapter 6) that we find in puritanical periods in certain times and places in all the major world (i.e. written) religions and cultures; and sometimes in others.

If we take seriously those accounts of world development which over the long term see the east as static, the west as dynamic – and even Braudel takes this line in his great synthesis on *Civilization and Capitalism, 15th–18th Century*, the first volume of which is entitled *The Structures of Everyday Life*[12] – that coincidence seems surprising. Or if one subscribes to the doctrines of 'Asiatic exceptionalism' or 'Oriental despotism', they would appear to inhibit this development of urban tastes – because urban they largely were.

These observations about parallelisms imply that one society in the major Eurasian complex was able at times to acquire some competitive advantage over the others, as some would possibly argue is the case at present in relation to globalization of some 'fast foods' – MacDonald's, KFC and even Coca-Cola – though the Chinese were preparing tofu for sale at market places in the days of Marco Polo. An advantage was certainly present in China with the invention of printing and the use of paper, both of which greatly increased the speed and accuracy of the circulation of knowledge, including medico-culinary knowledge. But in broad terms, urban cultures and the accompanying mercantile and manufacturing activities developed *pari passu* in the history of both east and west, with supremacy applying first to one sphere and then another.

It is true that, after the fall of the Roman Empire, or perhaps after the Islamic dominance of Mediterranean trade – the question of which has been usefully discussed by the archaeologists Hodges and Whitehouse, who have attempted to modify the thesis of the historian Pirenne with the aid of archaeological material – there was certainly a decline of trade and of urban culture in the west, partly linked to the coming of Christianity, as the classicist Speiser[13] has argued in reference to some urban centres in the Byzantine world, where property was now given to the church rather than to the municipality. But the resultant stress on rural life, giving rise to the notion of feudalism, was a singularly western phenomenon which cannot, should not, be seen as a necessary phase of world history.

Elsewhere, Childe's urban civilization of the Bronze Age continued to produce a wider range of artisanal and manufactured objects, a wider set of trading networks, a greater development of mercantile culture. One step led to another in a series, in what he saw as 'social evolution'. Eventually, the west caught up again with the revival of trade and the growth of towns that Pirenne speaks of in the eleventh century. That took place because of the return of trade with the Near East where urban mercantile culture had never disappeared, a return in which the role of Venice[14] and other Italian centres was critical in relation to the east. Elsewhere in the world, trade networks had continued to extend from the Bronze Age, in Ceylon,[15] in south-east Asia,[16] in the Near East,[17] and the Indian Ocean.[18] Eventually, Christian Europe caught up with the 'modernizing' process, often by borrowing from the east, for example with printing, paper, porcelain, cotton, silk weaving, the compass and gun powder, foods such as citrus, tea and sugar, many species of flowers; it developed the process of industrial manufacture (as well as the manufacture of ships and armaments) and in the nineteenth century gained an impressive comparative advantage. No sooner had it done so than industrial 'capitalism' began to spread to those other parts of the world where the urban cultures of the Bronze Age were already most developed (and by migration too).

Archaeologists are used to dealing with parallel and alternate developments of this kind, since that is the course of prehistory. Broadly there are two ways of accounting for the fact the societies throughout the world have developed in this way, which nineteenth-century anthropologists referred to by the now old-fashioned and discredited terms 'diffusion' and 'independent invention'. But although the terms are unfashionable, the process is crucial. Independent invention can better be seen as the working out of the logical possibilities of any one 'stage', the gradual elaboration of cultures, especially urban, over time. 'Diffusion' can be thought of in terms of patterns of communication, particularly important in mercantile cultures that were always engaged in exchanging goods with one another, and hence in the communication of knowledge. This latter process was significant for the transfer of certain types of information from one part of the globe to another, as paradigmatically was the case with the manufacture of sugar, in what Braudel calls 'its conquest of the world'.[19] That transfer very much affected the nature of taste and the structure of recipes everywhere. But by and large, unlike the ingredients, the structure of the major cuisines was not subject to the same process of 'diffusion' until recently under globalization; today, when Chinese and Indian restaurants are found in so many places around the world, their presence also affects the nature of home-cooking as well. But this process is different from the movement of food crops or animal species. Basically these cuisines, including the *hautes cuisines*, emerged *in situ* by a process of logical development from earlier forms, a formalization of Neolithic consumption under the conditions of class differentiation and urban life, where social eating took on a new importance and where food served to distinguish one class or one culture from another. People maintained a particular structure of life, developed in a national context (a single language – at least, written – a national communications network in schools and through publication), which they took with them abroad.

I have tried very sketchily to put down my thoughts relating to the Urban Revolution, to 'civilization', to the emergence of differentiated cuisines, and to broach the question which this raises of the parallel development of the major Eurasian societies towards industrial capitalism by way of the mercantile variety. This was gradually developed, at roughly the same tempo, in different parts of that landmass. In doing so, I have tried to link up historical developments with prehistorical ones, a completely necessary but much neglected task, seeing the broad parallelism partly in terms of internal 'logical' development and partly in terms of the continual communication that existed between mercantile cultures.

In a certain number of these cultures you find a yet more differentiated cuisine, a 'high' cuisine. China, France and Italy would be examples, but also the Arabic cuisine (certainly the Turkish) and in India, possibly in Mexico, too. The characteristic of a high cuisine, as distinct from a differentiated cuisine and cooking more generally, is the stimulation of connoisseurship, so that the food is not simply 'higher' but 'luxurious' – though in this and other respects there has been a decline since classical times – created for an expert clientele, usually by male cooks rather than by female wives, perhaps elaborated in cook-books or in accounts such as that of Trimalchio's banquet (in Petronius' *Satyricon*) in ancient Rome, and above all subject to discussion and criticism. That communication assumes a self-conscious class, knowledgeable about food and drink, discussing its qualities at banquets, even cultivating a written literature about food. Obviously, the situation required an educated, leisured clientele, educated at least in the preparation and consumption of food, a clientele of the kind that the sinologist K. C. Chang[20] describes for the Northern Song capital, at least by the twelfth century, when literati-bureaucrats gathered there and formalized Chinese regional cooking by demanding sophisticated versions of their own local dishes. Or in Paris at Louis XIV's court at Versailles, where aristocrats (and the *haute bourgeoisie*) came from all corners of France to spend part of the time there at the king's behest.

It was this degree of elaboration that, both in the west and earlier in the east, also produced the highest level of restaurant culture, the Tours d'Argent of this world. That shift of food preparation outside the homes of the bourgeoisie and of the aristocracy was the preliminary to the move from restricted luxury cultures to those of mass consumption that slowly followed the Industrial Revolution. The development of restaurant cultures was clearly earlier in China than the west, where scrolls already show a variety of public eating and drinking places at the time of Marco Polo. At a less exalted level, food, in the shape of tofu, was available for purchase in the markets. Long before this time a highly differentiated cuisine had emerged, making use of lacquered bowls and chopsticks which were found in graves as early as 3000 BCE.[21] Europe in the medieval period offered little apart from the inns, over-night stopping places that catered for wayfarers.

Even with the spread of mass culture, some differentiation continued to exist since variations in income control expenditure, but the gap has been greatly reduced, at least within particular communities. A similar process has obviously taken place with regard to clothing, which at one stage was subject to sumptuary laws, restricting forms of costume to certain classes or roles; then, much later, it became dominated by fashion[22] as the rich bourgeoisie made their presence increasingly felt, giving way to the contemporary pattern of the mass consumption of similar styles by the employed community in general.

By fashion I refer to the regular turnover in style, which may have been developed in Lyon in the seventeenth century around the activity of aristocrats at the French court in Versailles. Not that change in clothing began with that movement, but it was intermittent and only really developed with the silk industry.[23]

Eurasia and the Bronze Age

While these processes have proceeded more rapidly in some major societies in Eurasia than in others, the overall movement has been widespread. Archaeologists are used to facing large transitions of this kind, for example from the Mesolithic to the Neolithic. They tend to look for explanations, when they give them, in terms either of external communication or of structural similarities arising internally from a parallel initial situation. Because of their interest in cultures, anthropologists are likely to look for more specific, but still very general, factors, as are historians and to some extent sociologists – frequently to mentalities for example. In my view this latter is dangerous territory for these scholars, and even more dangerous for the archaeologist who has fewer data to go on. Explanations based on culture or on mentalities may be misleading if they entail the conceiving of temporary difference as a permanent frame. We need also to take into account that, as with the differentiated and *haute cuisine*, or with fashion, some developments have run parallel in different post-Bronze Age cultures over the long term, even if at somewhat different times. This has not been a question of globalization, as often understood: today, in effect, westernization. It represents the growth of urban, bourgeois society, which has been developing continually ever since the times of which Childe was writing, partly by interacting with other societies, partly by internal 'logic'. For these were merchant cultures, engaged in creating products and services which they would exchange with the local countryside but also with each other. In their nature they constituted 'ports of trade', to use an expression from Karl Polanyi but in a different way. They were making commodities, providing services, and from time to time improving those products and services, not always standing still. They were engaged in manufacture and trade to earn a living, which meant they had to make a profit (or at least break even), not make a loss.

These activities should be seen as the roots of capitalism, at least of mercantile capitalism. They also led to 'the sprouts of capitalism' as these have been designated by some Chinese scholars. At this level, there is no problem about the origin of capitalism and the growth of urban cultures in all their many socio-cultural forms, including the arts. The great leap in our thinking comes when we realize that, whatever has taken place with the mass media of recent times, the west was not the inventor of these arts, literature (the novel for example), the theatre, painting or sculpture, much less of a special set of values that permitted modernization to come about there and nowhere else. These activities have been developing throughout the urban societies of the Eurasian continent, sometimes one taking the lead, sometimes another. But in the 'feudal' period, the west fell distinctly behind and had to recover by means of a rebirth, a Renaissance, which revived and expanded the culture of earlier times.

I have spoken of the broad base of mercantile capitalism; that seems obvious given the extent of early merchant activities in Asia and the export of Indian cotton goods to the East Indian islands (Indonesia) and to south-east Asia (Indo-China), as well as the export of Chinese bronzes, silks and porcelain throughout those regions. Compared to western Europe and even to the Mediterranean, the Far East was a hive of mercantile activity. According to the anthropological sinologist Francesca Bray, China remained the greatest economic power in the world until the end of the eighteenth century.[24] What about manufacture, and even industry, which are rightly seen as the key features of modern capitalism? Such widespread exchange already involved manufactures. Silk was largely but not entirely produced domestically, though it was collected by the state and marketed by merchants.[25] But ceramics are described by the sinologist and art historian Ledderose as industrial,[26] making use of a complex division of labour, of modular production and of a factory-type organization.[27] Nor was it only ceramics that were subject to industrial techniques. In India, as in China, textiles were produced largely on a domestic basis, often organized by merchants under the putting-out systems and cottage industry as in proto-industrial Europe. But there were also large factory-type institutions, such as the *karkhanas*, cloth manufactories, of the Mughal emperors.[28] In China, a more impressive example was the very important paper industry. Mills developed around the beginning of the Common Era in different parts of the country, providing a cheaper writing material than silk, skins (parchment) or papyrus – in Europe, expensively imported from Egypt – since it could be made out of cheap local materials. Paper manufacture spread throughout the Muslim world and eventually reached western Europe in time for the printing revolution (coming first to Spain and to Italy from Sicily). The presence of this industrially manufactured, mass-produced, cheap material for writing meant that, until Gutenberg with his printing press, the circulation of information and ideas was much more rapid and extensive in the east than in the west.

In matters of cooking and cuisine, we have seen that the urban cultures of the east certainly did not lag behind the west. Eating out is a key feature of the modern industrial world; we know about the development of the restaurant in France after the Revolution when aristocratic households could no longer employ full-time cooks who took up catering for the public instead, though the case has been slightly exaggerated. China had an advanced restaurant culture at least as early as the visit of the Italian merchant Marco Polo, in the thirteenth century. It also had in effect the mass production of take-away food in the shape of tofu being sold in the markets to transient eaters. And tea (*chai*), of course, provided them with a liquid equivalent. In Europe that kind of provision, particularly for the working classes, had to await the nineteenth century and the massive importation of Chinese and Indian tea and of American (originally Indian) sugar to feed the new proletariat working in the factories of northern England.[29] Sugar had reached China from India many centuries before.

That situation reflects the fact that, throughout the major societies of Eurasia, urban cultures represented a continuous development from those of the Bronze Age. There were interruptions, due to ecological, economic and military factors – invasions of 'barbarism', disruptions of commerce, failures of government. But overall, urban cultures developed in complexity over the centuries, in relation to production, exchange, distribution, finance, as well as in material and intellectual life. We see that process with regard to the preparation and consumption of food. In this and on the wider, socio-economic scene, in the arts, in education, in commerce and in manufacture, historians of human culture need to make a link between the evidence from the Bronze Age and that from the post-classical period, leading up to industrial capitalism itself. The continuity has been disastrously fractured by a concentration on European experience alone.

5

Merchants and their role
in alternation

All this exchange that was at the basis of the spread of Bronze Age culture, immaterial as well as material, had of course a human agency in the shape of merchants (in contrast to simple conquest and migration). Their activity expanded as the economy and culture expanded but it was central in human life itself. In behavioural terms, exchange is a feature of many primate societies; you groom my back, I'll groom yours. Nor of course is that exchange confined only to primates. Among other species the exchange of goods and services is rarer, but it does occur. Food may be exchanged for sexual favours, as in the fictional account of the incident between the male and female guinea fowl in the Bagre recital of the LoDagaa of northern Ghana: the male finds a bean flower but refuses to share it with his mate, saying 'last night you refused me sex, today I refuse you food'.[1] That is a common situation in local cultures too.

So it is hardly surprising early human communities engaged in an elaborate exchange of goods and services with their neighbours. The exchange of services often means the exchange of like for like, which is usually described as 'reciprocal behaviour'. Such behaviour may seem superfluous from a narrowly practical standpoint, as when a lineage among the LoDagaa calls upon neighbours to carry out some of the cleansing rituals after a death. However, such arrangements – of which there are many, including 'joking partnerships' – clearly establish a network of ties with adjacent groups that serve to mitigate any dispute that may arise between them. The same is true of marriage. Most simple agricultural societies practice exogamy, marriage out, with their neighbours. As the anthropologist E. B. Tylor stated, 'Primitive man was faced with the alternative of marrying out or being killed out.' Nor was such behaviour entirely confined within any particular 'tribal' group. Marriage and reciprocal behaviour generally could occur across the boundaries, including linguistic ones.

These examples of the exchange of services are very local. Much wider systems of exchange existed even very early on, regarding goods and ideas. Even in hunter-gatherer societies in North America, we find the exchange of abalone shells from the coast of California with rabbit skins from the interior, crossing many tribal and linguistic barriers in the process.[2] Or in Europe, we find the appearance of Baltic amber in the Mediterranean in the Palaeolithic period. Subsequently, such exchange systems expanded, giving rise to a special category of long-distance merchant as well as to the local traders, often women – 'market women' in contemporary west Africa. In recent centuries, a virtually Neolithic Africa has imported millions of cowry shells from the Maldives in the Indian Ocean, which it uses for exchange purposes on an intertribal basis. In the same way, gold has crossed the Sahara by commercial routes, as have slaves, salt and many other products. The example I like to cite is the pewter ewer with the personal arms of Richard II of England turning up in a war-shrine in the Asante capital of Kumasi, having arrived by trade routes across the desert.

The Neolithic period was followed by the Bronze Age around 3000 BCE. As we have seen, that has been called the Urban Revolution and saw a great development in plough agriculture as well as in urban crafts. The new towns and their craft activities often involved the import of raw materials, especially metals (following the Bronze Age), not only of

Merchants and their role in alternation

luxury materials in long-distance trade but of many local products too. Such exchange was sometimes carried out on a tributary basis, as at times in China. It might also be subject to unequal power relations, to forced exchange, as in some colonial or conquest situation where an invading army takes what it wants and leaves no more than a pittance in return. But in general it occurs between more or less freely consenting adults who are at liberty to work out their own profits and their losses. We see this very clearly in the trade between Assyria and Kanesh in Anatolia, excellently analysed by the Scandinavian orientalist Larsen.[3] This was a literate society and the accounts were kept in writing, one of its earliest uses in the Near East. Indeed the French historian Schmandt-Besserat sees the very origin of writing in the use of tokens for trading purposes, which led eventually to the making of the clay envelopes (*bullae*) that contained the units involved in a specific transaction. Later on, the tokens were replaced by marks on the envelopes, signs of what should have been within.[4] However this may have been, writing was certainly of primary importance for the more elaborate trading transactions that Bronze Age society involved (and co-evolved).

These complex transactions meant that specialist merchants also traded very widely, while other members of the community worked in local markets. We have early evidence of precious stones being brought from Afghanistan to the Near East and many other long-distance transfers of material objects. But, apart from the goods themselves, these transactions also led to contact between different cultures, between speakers of different languages who may well have employed a *lingua franca* as traders frequently did at a later date. In this way, not only goods but information and knowledge got exchanged, including knowledge of how to prepare the goods exchanged. So that, in certain ways, distant cultures imitated others and changed in similar directions – subject to some attempts at delaying the transfer of 'valuable' knowledge – by diffusion as well as by parallel social evolution; for example a new form of a tool might develop following a certain logic of 'the next step'. One of the extraordinary things about the history of humanity is the way that stage has followed stage – the early Palaeolithic by middle Palaeolithic – all over the world.[5] Unless one has recourse to some mystical theory, that process can only have happened through parallel social evolution, the 'logic' of development ('independent invention' in the earlier phraseology), and through diffusion, in which trade and exchange more generally played an important role. Even in the Stone Age, better flint was available in one place, such as Grimes Graves in East Anglia, than in another, as was also the case in the later Mediterranean.[6] Trade was essential to the growth of human life from the earliest times, including the institution of the market and the rise of some specialist individuals (later merchants).[7]

Come the Urban Revolution, mercantile activity becomes much extended. Specialist occupations proliferate in towns, such as those of the bakers of bread and the weavers of cloth. They operate from separate quarters and, while some of their product may be commanded by the court or the temple on which they depend for redistribution, the bulk is offered to fellow citizens for sale. For rarer items, long-distance trade develops, with merchants travelling away from home for months and establishing bases in other countries, like the quarter of Chinese merchants found in tenth-century Baghdad, the Indian sugar merchants Marco Polo found in the southern Song capital, or the activities of Europeans like Polo himself, for that matter. The Silk Road was but one channel for this long-distance exchange, one that supplied the Romans with silk cloth and the Topkapi palace in Istanbul with fine porcelain. Indians too traded very widely, as did Armenians in the other direction. It was not all one way, even though Europeans tend to think of themselves as having first 'discovered' and 'explored' the world. Think of the long voyages of Cheng He and, earlier, of the shipwrecked Indian sailor on the Egyptian coast.[8] Indeed the Indian Ocean was crisscrossed by trade routes at least from the third millennium BCE (with Mesopotamia). It was subsequently the route

Merchants and their role in alternation

taken by many Near Eastern traders, Jews, Christians (beginning with St Thomas) and Muslims, with the Romans at Muzaris and Arikemedu, all of whom traded with south India and settled on the Malabar Coast. Merchants were obviously also money-men. They had to exchange different types of goods and information, and this often required a neutral medium of exchange-money, perhaps shells, later metal, and even later paper. That meant they accumulated exchange capacity that they might eventually use to rival the landed aristocracy, commissioning great houses and works of art, as well as indulging in an elaborate cuisine and a complex lifestyle. They developed their own culture, their own drama (as in Japan), their own educational institutions since they were concerned their young should learn the tools of their trade, the use of writing and arithmetic for keeping accounts and other aspects of a literate education. At the same time they were often constrained by the dominant religions, whose practitioners were experts in the written word. The power of their money and their influence over production and exchange activity meant they had an increasing part to play in commissioning (and in creating) literary works, paintings, drama and music, many of which in the longer term had a non-religious element and benefited from their more secular interest. In this way they created an urban culture that increasingly reflected their own dominant role in society.

At the same time the culture of luxury did not have it all its own way. Merchants were interested in money and had to save as well as spend. There was a strong element of asceticism, as Weber pointed out, and as we will see in the next chapter this attribute was not confined to the Protestant Reformation but was found more widely.

I emphasize the reciprocal growth of mercantile activity from the Bronze Age onwards, especially between the 'urban civilizations', since it serves to counter one of the major errors of western scholars regarding the belief in the unbroken development of human society. There is general agreement among prehistorians about the general progress of humankind until the Bronze Age. But with literacy, with history, matters get more complicated. In antiquity, Europe is held to diverge from this common heritage. The Greeks and the Romans created a new order, based on slavery and democracy (for some Greek citizens), which left Asia distinct and indeed behind. Looking back at the history of Eurasia teleologically from the standpoint of the undoubted advantage they achieved in a variety of spheres in the nineteenth century, scholars and public alike have searched for reasons for the western development of 'capitalism' back in time, back to European antiquity, back to feudalism and then to the Renaissance. For example, towns are widely thought to have developed differently in Asia and Europe, as did economic transactions. The western town grew up in the medieval period and in a way that was held to be very different from elsewhere.[9]

In the main, Braudel sees market activity and its associated production as being characteristic of both Europe and Asia; each is characterized by capitalism in this broad sense. However, only the west achieved 'true capitalism', that is, finance capitalism, in which merchants and producers invested their profits back into industry on a large scale, achieving that continuous growth (the take-off) which many have seen as the main characteristic of 'modern capitalism' and as associated with a different mentality, the restless search for gain.[10] Most commentators are less generous, insisting that only the west invented 'capitalism', the east being the subject of 'Asiatic exceptionalism'.

But up until the time of the Industrial Revolution, there was nothing intrinsic about the east that inhibited mercantile – that is, capitalist – activity. Merchants continuously traded reciprocally between east and west; urban civilizations developed by invention and by diffusion in a roughly parallel fashion. That was in the nature of merchant existence. Moreover, these persons necessarily invested part of their profit back into their enterprise as capital, for new ships or for new manufacturing material, each time trying to improve upon the old. It is true that the overall organization of trade might not necessarily be undertaken by the merchants themselves, although they would always be involved at a lower level. The provision of ships (or other means of transport) or even of part of the goods to be exchanged might be made by the state or by another 'great organization', such as a temple or church, or even by a collective body of merchants. As with differences in production, this happened in both the west and the east. But in many ways the effects were not necessarily dissimilar, as we see from contemporary Japan, China, or formerly in the Soviet Union, although under some circumstances one method might produce better results than another. But 'capital' always had to be accumulated and invested in merchants and mercantile activity as well as in production.

Let us start, not teleologically from a form of social or economic organization called 'capitalism', which is claimed to have appeared only in the west, but by looking at the common basis of Bronze Age activity, in which we find urban civilizations (and rural societies too) that traded between themselves; their manufacturers produced more of certain items than were needed (sometimes these were not used locally at all, like Asante kolanuts) and were exchanged by means of merchants and their transport, with others, far and near. In the manufacturing and in the trading spheres, these activities gradually grew more complex over time, stimulated both internally and externally. All involved the accumulation and investment of capital but that investment obviously increased with the greater complexity involved in the manufacture of the objects of trade. By the time of the Industrial Revolution, huge factories and large amounts of capital and non-human energy were required in order to produce the great variety of objects that the masses increasingly required in a consumer society. But that point, which Braudel calls finance or true capitalism, was reached in the course of a process of production and exchange that began centuries before, not only in various parts of Eurasia.

Everywhere productivity increased, for example mechanization may be said to have begun with the loom. Non-human energy was harnessed by water and wind. Weaving and processing textiles became increasingly complicated, involving the use of water power in China in the twelfth century to power reeling machines for hemp. Similar machines were later developed in Italy for reeling silk thread, so similar in fact that the historian Elvin thinks there must have been some westward diffusion of the technique.

Not only mechanization but factories too appeared in various parts of the world well before the Industrial Revolution. There were centres in China for the large-scale production of silk; paper-making required water power and often large-scale production. The manufacture of porcelain involved all the criteria laid down by Adam Smith concerning the division of labour. Nor was China the only country that produced mass-goods for markets that were serviced by long-distance merchants. The Indians also made and exported cotton goods in bulk quantities.

In other words, without making use of the nineteenth-century English concept of 'capitalism', we can conceive of the continuous growth of manufacturing and mercantile activity, mainly in urban contexts but always associated with rural societies. That growth was partly internal, the result of inventions which were developments from the previous position, derived from the logic of the situation, and partly external by diffusion from other cultures, especially by trade and the surrounding activity of merchants. The exchanging of goods and knowledge led to their production by artisans and manufacturers elsewhere (and to primary producers in the case of raw materials), the complexity of which grew over time, gradually but exponentially. Each step in this process meant an increase in producers, in merchants, in all the associated activities of shop-keepers, accountants (and money-men), lawyers (and the law), artists (and the arts) of various kinds. Towns expanded, and with them administration and the two 'great organizations', the armed forces and the 'church', or religious institutions more generally. At the core lay the growth of the town-dwelling middle class, the bourgeoisie. It did not require the advent of something called capitalism (in the restricted sense) to produce such a 'class'.

Merchants and their role in alternation

It required only economic differentiation. They existed in all urban communities and their role expanded as trade and manufacture expanded, at the expense of other groups, until they and their activities eventually dominated the society, which was no longer entirely dependent on primary production and the agricultural sphere.

Such an account, based primarily on mercantile exchange, gives us a less fractured view of developments in the west and does not separate those from the east, which played an intrinsic part in this process. In other words, it helps to eliminate European ethnocentrism and teleological history. It also helps to explain the very considerable parallelisms in cultural developments in the west and the east – especially, as we have seen, in the culture of food and of flowers, as well as in the arts more generally. It also implies a series of parallel achievements in science and in written knowledge more widely, leading to an alternation first favouring one culture, then another, as we see happening in the situation of China today which is rapidly becoming, once again, the 'workshop of the world', which involves the interlinking activities of manufacture and trade, both of which mean the investment of capital and knowledge on a large scale.

6

Merchant wealth and puritanical asceticism

We have spoken of the role of merchants and manufacturers in the creation of wealth in exchange, both internally and also externally. But at the same time much of the discussion of the supposed emergence of capitalism in the west has centred upon Weber's treatment of ascetic Protestantism; this was clearly associated with the presence of Christianity, even of Judaeo-Christian civilization, or Abrahamistic monotheism, forgetting that there are three major religions descended from Abraham, the third being, of course, Islam. This view is not confined to Weber but, in the Baechler volume, marks the contributions of Mann, Macfarlane, Hall and others as well.[1] But we have always to remember the restraint and denial that accompanied the accumulation of merchant wealth in and before the Renaissance.

My aim here is to generalize what I have called the puritanical complex so that it is understood as a feature of many post-Bronze Age societies that have become in some respects cultures of luxury, at least for the favoured few. But I see some aspects of this complex as being characteristic more widely of all human society, even beyond the confines of that period. And I begin with the possibility of understanding both the presence and absence of art, especially figurative art, from this point of view. In this

Merchant wealth and puritanical asceticism

review I look at not only 'luxury' societies but also some non-literate ones.

There are two main approaches to a work of art, an evaluation (appreciation and criticism) and a socio-historical analysis, apart that is from a set of comments (including philosophical ones) on life and representation to which a particular work gives rise and which I view as a variety of *belles lettres*. I do not think that the social sciences can be of much help in the first but in the second they can – more obviously with regard to anthropology and non-European art but there are also questions of cultural history which are raised. I want to consider the most inclusive of such questions, which is the absence of art, or at least of figurative art.

There are interesting differences between societies in the use of sculpture, and of figurative representations. The Senufo of the Ivory Coast have a very strong tradition of woodcarving that continues until today, even though to some extent influenced by the coming of Islam. Their neighbours, the 'Lobi' of Goua, have much less (among the Senufo even the kitchen utensils are carved); they have some masks, not of very high quality, which stylistically they have borrowed from the Baule to the south. Further to the east, the LoDagaa have very much less. No masks at all, except those they import to present to visiting dignitaries; some ancestral shrines of vaguely anthropomorphic shape (*saa daa*) and some poorly carved figures (*betibe*) which are used in conjunction with cults to the beings of the wild and similar low-level figures; and there are some mud sculptures of shrines. The nearby Tallensi have even less.

But in museums of African art you cannot show absence, even if only of some category of shrine. There are in fact gaps of whole cultures as well as in topics within cultures, where there is no representation – not figurative, anyhow. A museum shows only presence, just as art history shows only continuity. What is not shown is silence, blanks, gaps.

However, is it possible we are dealing not simply with neutral phenomena but with deliberate avoidance, with a rejection? Clearly, in western cultures we often do reject art, especially in what is generally referred to as puritanism, though in using this word I am not confining myself to religious refusals to adopt figurative representation.

I start therefore with doubts about art, all art. The problem was posed in Marcel Proust's account of Bergotte's death after visiting an exhibition to remind himself of Vermeer's *View of Delft*: 'He passed in front of a number of paintings and was struck by the dryness and pointlessness of an art devoted to the counterfeit, work so much less than the breeze and sunshine on a Venetian palace.'[2] In *Representations and Contradictions*,[3] I have suggested that similar objections to representation are a potential feature of all human societies at one time or another. That also applies to other 'aesthetic' features. In the *Culture of Flowers*,[4] I saw the rejection of their use in some societies and at specific historical periods as also being trans-cultural, although concentrated in the luxury cultures originating in the Bronze Age where the growing of domesticated flowers began. The same seemed to be true of objections to the development of elaborate foods, discussed in *Cooking, Cuisine and Class*.[5] Elsewhere, I have discussed wine from a similar perspective.[6]

The features treated then were flowers, food, wine, images, theatre, fiction (specifically the novel), relics and representations of sexuality. What I hinted at but did not really discuss was that these rejections, prohibitions or avoidances tended to overlap: where you found one, the others were often present. Was there then the possibility of a 'puritanical complex', with not all the features being present at one time but with a significant cluster emerging together? Let us take a context in which the world 'puritan' originated, and specifically the Scottish Presbyterian variety. Flowers were not a great feature of the Scottish landscape in earlier times, where the giving of cut flowers was quite a rare event. Even today the number of florists in Scotland is proportionally much less than in England, and there again much less than in France. Flowers were not normally a feature of social giving. Indeed, the saying of a Scottish woman of my mother's generation was: 'I'd rather ha'e eggs.' Equally, Scottish cemeteries, while

Merchant wealth and puritanical asceticism

not altogether devoid of flowers, bear a strong resemblance to the Protestant graveyards of New England in their virtual barrenness. Flowers, particularly cut flowers, are viewed as an unnecessary luxury on which good money should not be wasted. But for cemeteries it was not only a moral problem but a theological one, since to place flowers on a grave might be construed as an attempt to persuade the ancestors to intervene on one's behalf. And in a strongly monotheistic religion, that would have been blasphemy.

However, it was not only flowers but also food. Here there was undoubtedly a difference, as to some extent with flowers, between the behaviour of upper groups and that of the middle and lower classes. The latter often considered high living, in the shape of elaborate foods or expensive wines (indeed, sometimes, any alcohol), as luxuries with which one should dispense in the interests of one's own income (or health) or of giving to the church or to the poor. Of course, for the poor there was little question of such elaboration, although in Scotland standards were generally low. Fortune, who was sent out to Hong Kong and China as a plant collector for the London Botanical Society in the 1840s, was led to remark how much better the ordinary Chinese ate than their equivalents in Scotland.

Not all Scotland was equally abstemious. While the poor ate poorly, the middle classes modestly, the rich did not spare themselves, though the manner of preparation certainly fell short of the Chinese. Regarding drink, there was a different dichotomy. The rich imported wines and spirits from France, legally or illegally. But Scotland was also the great place for producing whisky. However, restrictions were placed upon its consumption. Taverns, inns, public houses were not places visited by respectable God-fearing people. The hours of consumption were restricted. On Sundays one had to have travelled at least five miles in order to be able to get an alcoholic drink. In fact, many families firmly rejected their consumption, whether in the house or outside. I do not remember any alcohol ever appearing in my mother's house on the borders of what were then the counties of Aberdeen and Banff, although important distilleries were situated nearby which contributed greatly to the region's economy. Even when she moved south to the London area at the age of sixteen, the only alcohol she allowed herself for medicinal purposes was brandy, putting it on the same level as heroin or laudanum.

Regarding images and other forms of representation, their history in Scotland was as extreme as in other extreme Protestant groups of the period. In the religious sphere, they were virtually abandoned. Pictures and sculptures vanished from churches, as did stained glass windows. Existing ones were destroyed; the new no longer created. Cemeteries were emptied of figurative embellishment. So a whole profession disappeared, possibly migrating elsewhere or working in the secular domain. But the secular did not fare all that much better. Illustrations were permitted for children, especially to lead them into moral literature. That literature itself played down fiction, or at least romance, the fantasy world as distinct from the realistic; both had to have a moral dimension. For adults, little value was placed on fiction (except 'history' with Walter Scott) and even less on drama. At the end of the Middle Ages, the town of Edinburgh had been a centre of poetic and dramatic activity: in poetry, there was the great achievement of Dunbar; for the drama, Lindsay wrote *The Thrie Estaitis* in 1540. But after the Reformation no play was produced on the Edinburgh stage for some 200 years. The festivals of All Saints and All Souls were abolished. In England the very Protestant ceremony of Guy Fawkes on 5 November, the celebration of the failure of the Catholic plot to blow up Parliament, took its place (as in the southern United States), while in Scotland, no lover of the English Parliament, it was Hallowe'en, the eve of All Saints, that became a children's party, associated with elves and with goblins.

As for the other elements in my hypothetical model, that is, relics and representations of sexuality, the cult of relics was obviously set aside by the Protestant church as it broke away from the Catholic; indeed, that was one of its originating characteristics. Sexuality too was always under pressure; although some extreme breakaway churches (such as the

Anabaptists and the Mormons), following the Biblical model of the Old Testament, led a revival of polygyny, the main emphasis on family values was of a more restrictive kind, with strong sanctions against adultery.

New England shared much of the same ideology and practice as Scotland, following the time of John Knox. They had the same iconophobia, the same anti-theatrical prejudices, and all recreation was focused on 'sober mirth', with no ball games, cards or dice, with modest dressing and generally restrained behaviour. That behaviour was modified towards the end of the seventeenth century but certain restrictions remained until the time of the Revolution against British rule. Theatre only achieved legitimacy in New England in the last decade of the eighteenth century. The same changes had taken place earlier in England with the return to the throne (the Restoration) of the Stuarts after the Cromwellian Commonwealth.

New England was a highly literate society: in the founding generation, approximately two-thirds of the men and one-third of the women could read. By the revolutionary decade, the figures had risen to include all men and 80 per cent of women. Belief in the virtues of the written word was very strong and many books were imported. The iconophobia that made most other forms of art difficult for puritans to appreciate posed no ideological problem for the written word itself. In fact they allowed illustrations to the Bible, preferring for that reason the Genesis Bible of 1660 to the King James version. But what they read was overwhelmingly religious, though this source was supplemented at the end of the seventeenth century by puritanical captivity tales, which became more secular in the second quarter of the following century. Confessional tales of famous criminals followed a similar course. Only in the middle of the eighteenth century did the novel become the dominant literary form. Romances were particularly popular with women but continued to be criticized by the hierarchy; in 1693 Increase Mather wrote of the 'vast mischief of false notions and images of things, particularly of love and honour'.[7] During the eighteenth century,

The Eurasian Miracle

'moral arbiters continued to frown on all fiction'; representations of reality were out.

Turning to the features of our general model, we have touched upon images, theatre and fiction; others were food and wine, flowers, relics and sexuality. Food was a matter of restraint in New England, as in Cromwellian England and in Scotland; its consumption was part of 'sober' enjoyment, avoiding excess.[8] Flowers too were treated warily, especially in religious contexts where they might be taken as offerings to the dead. They were offensive on these religious grounds, but also because to some they represented 'luxury', the culture of the leisured classes. Relics of saints and martyrs were anathema not only to puritans but to all Protestants, being roundly condemned by Luther for cheating people out of their money. The festival of All Saints disappeared, as did many other celebrations of patron saints. But the reaction to religious festivities did not stop there; Christmas disappeared, as in Scotland, to give way to the secular Hogmanay, while regular celebrations were replaced by what were at first irregular Thanksgivings to God for blessings bestowed. Guy Fawkes Day, also called Pope's Day, was celebrated in early New England and that eventually led to a modification of the puritan attachment to 'sober mirth', since it became an occasion that could lead to boisterous behaviour.

All the major Near Eastern religions included an array of puritanical attitudes. Islam has been the most persistent, especially regarding the aversion to images, above all in sculpture. But it has likewise objected to the theatre, to fiction, to secular music and to sexual licence. In theatre, the exception was the miracle play of Husain performed by Shi'ites; but, as with similar performances in medieval Europe, this play evaded the general ban because it was religious in inspiration and partook of a ritual rather than a theatrical performance; these two genres may be formally similar (as maintained in 'performance-theory') but from the actor's viewpoint they were totally different.

Images, either two- or three-dimensional, are condemned by the main Islamic traditions; they made their way into

Merchant wealth and puritanical asceticism

Safavid Persia from contact with the Chinese along the Silk Route, and thence into Mughal India, where two-dimensional paintings were common but where Hindu three-dimensional sculpture was defaced as being pagan, not simply because it was Hindu but because all sculpture was objectionable to the Creator. So too were relics, which again could be worshipped instead of God. Storytelling also had its dangers, as presenting something other than the truth, which was paramount.

There was some breach in these prohibitions. Exceptions were found mainly at court, in the early palaces with their elaborate mosaics; to some extent with the cedars of Lebanon decorating merchants' houses; certainly with tales such as appeared in 'The Thousand and One Nights'. Some figurative representation went on at the local level, as well as some oral storytelling; disapproval might be strong but representation was always knocking at the gate and had to be repelled by reference to canonical beliefs.

Judaism had similar traditions to Islam; indeed, they flowed from the same source. The absence of images is the best-known. As in Islam, it was sacrilegious to make a figurative representation of God. With very few exceptions, there were no Jewish painters before the Russian artist Marc Chagall, who had to come to Paris to paint. The Godhead and his creations could not be imaged, even in words, according to the Spanish philosopher Moses Maimonides. Drama was equally objectionable. Some have argued that this was the result of spectacles in the Roman theatre where Jews, like Christians, had been cruelly portrayed (as later in *The Merchant of Venice*) or in the arena where they had to combat wild animals. But once again the objections were more general, more profound, to any form of theatrical representation, though in the Middle Ages they did copy the Christian Miracle plays at the festival of Purim enacting the Biblical story of Esther. But, as with the Shi'ite plays about Husain and the Christian miracle plays themselves, this entry into drama was made under a religious umbrella, as ritual rather than theatre, like the Christian Passion Play.

What is essential for my thesis is to realize that these features are not permanent aspects of a group's cultural tradition. It was the very same people, the Jews, who rejected theatre and the visual arts and yet in the USA became so overwhelmingly dominant in these spheres. Puritanism in these various respects was tied to a specific set of religious beliefs. When they wavered or changed, a complete switch took place.

It would be surprising if the third of this Trinity of Mediterranean religions, namely Christianity, did not display some similar characteristics, given its background in Judaism. Certainly, in the early stages, Christians showed strong iconophobic tendencies, above all with regard to three-dimensional sculpture. It virtually disappeared until the early Renaissance, when it returned in the Auvergne for example, and in 'Gothic' cathedrals. But even two-dimensional figurative representation had a difficult time, unless it was religious. The eighth-century iconoclastic movement was probably influenced by Islam but it all went back to earlier roots in Judaism. And even when images were permitted, they were religious and, in that sense, sanctified.

It was the same with the theatre, for there is evidence of a deliberate destruction of the Roman buildings. This meant that Christianity had encouraged the disappearance of the two great features of the artistic achievement of Greece and Rome – that is, its sculpture and its theatre.

Ritual was *not* an equivalent of dramatic performance, although it was in a sense an alternative. However, there was a gradual change regarding the arts with later Catholicism, manifest in the decoration of churches. The French priest Abbé Suger, combatting the 'puritanism' of the Cistercian Bernard of Clairvaux, claimed that God deserved only the most beautiful, the latter maintaining that worship should be of the simplest. Flowers were used, sculpture and stained glass adorned the temples. Many of the early Fathers of the Christian church had displayed a puritanism not simply for religious reasons, but because they were against luxury, against what they considered as unnecessary expenditure. This attitude was taken up again in many reform and protest movements against the established church. So that Protestants, but especially puritans, insisted upon a return to 'roots', to simplicity. In this spirit, they banished art from their churches in Holland as well as in Scotland and in New England.

So far I have written as if puritanism, rejectionism, was a European or Near Eastern phenomenon, an aspect of that tradition. So it is often treated, especially in studies relating to monotheism – there could be no alternatives to the worship of the one God. But that is untrue. It appears in aspects of Hinduism and Buddhism, and is found in both China and Japan. Indeed, elements of the complex are found even in non-literate societies. Not all earlier oral cultures were iconophile; not all worshipped images. Indeed in Africa there was rarely any image, even abstract, of the High God. He had no shrine like lesser divinities. There were other resistances too, not only to figuring some divinities (to figuring any in the case of the Tallensi of northern Ghana). But these absences do not get shown up in museums.

Presence and absence are very closely linked, at least in earlier times, by a series of doubts about the nature of figurative representations which are classically and most clearly expressed in the work of the Greek philosopher Plato. Representation was a lie, it was never the 'real thing', though for him the real thing was still an ideal. But that is true even in a more concrete sense. The picture of a 'horse' is never a horse. Nor is the word ever one either. This realization of the distance, consciously or unconsciously, may always give rise to doubts, and doubts to ambivalence, which is the almost inevitable outcome of man as a language-using animal, a representation-using animal coming face to face with the world, with his material and immaterial environment.

I say almost inevitable because, as the German essayist Walter Benjamin pointed out, since the advent of the rolling press we have been inundated with images, just as we have with fiction due to the vigorous diffusion of the novel, of films, of TV. Our earlier doubts have been swept aside.

The Eurasian Miracle

We live in a world of fiction, images and drama, a virtual reality which we have some difficulty in distinguishing from our own reality. We still put up some resistance to representations and may prefer abstract art, but earlier whole cultures refused to acknowledge figurative representation and opted for the abstract. You can see this in terms of the history of art.

In Mycenaean Crete, much art was definitely iconic, figurative, as in the well-known clay figures of a goddess, or in the later Minoan example from Cyprus from the eleventh century. That was followed in Greece by the Geometric period which began in Athens around 900 BCE, where it followed what has been called the Protogeometric style, especially of pottery. That was outstanding for its technical excellence, its elegance of shape, and its harmony and decoration.[9] The new art was dominated by 'logical order'.[10] The Geometric pottery was produced between c.900 and c.700 BCE and was characterized by abstract rectilinear designs which evolved from the Protogeometric phase in which the motifs were predominantly circular. The main vehicles for the decoration were funerary vases.

This pottery production took place in the so-called 'Dark Ages' which marked the gap between the presence of the Mycenaean script and the advent of the Phoenician alphabet. It would be wrong to think of it as being uniformly aniconic, but it was largely so. But Oriental master-craftsmen introduced figurative designs in imported wares, especially in precious metals (Persian art was primarily that of the goldsmith), leading to 'a strange ferment in the artistic sphere, which threw up some striking experiments in figured representations'.[11] However, in figurative art, 'there was no further progress until the generation just before the Dipylon Master', by the time of which work there was a significant increase in eastward exchanges. In rich Athenian burials (Middle Geometric II) from Anavysos we find two- and three-dimensional representations of horses, the artist getting to grips with the rendering of natural forms, 'a task so rarely attempted in the three previous centuries'.[12]

Merchant wealth and puritanical asceticism

What accounts for this shift to abstract and the return to figurative art? Cook points out that there had already been an abstract phase some 500 years earlier in the Middle Helladic. He goes on to say that it has been suggested that 'a natural taste for Geometric forms was inherent in the early population of Greece', which had been suppressed under the Mycenaean culture but emerged again when that collapsed; he himself prefers the notion that 'the ultimately Cretan characteristics of Mycenaean art had now been bred out'.[13] Others have seen the style as the product of an invading people.

The first two hypotheses see particular art forms as attached to particular populations over time, almost biologically ('naturally'); the third adapts a customary archaeological explanation of social change as resulting from invasion. All seem inadequate. It was also during this period that Greek burials shifted from cremation to inhumation (*c*.770–*c*.750 BCE) and then back again (*c*.700 BCE). Should we attempt to apply either of these types of explanation to this data? I think not.

I suggest we need to look in quite a different direction, one adopted by a Greek writer himself, namely Plato, in which case the 'Geometric' should be interpreted as the deliberate rejection of images, of figurative representation. I would argue that this is not only a possible, but a necessary, interpretation. Otherwise, one is involved in flaccid explanations of a 'cultural' shift from representation to abstract, which explains nothing as it omits any factor of human intentionality, of agency, and leaves causation in the hands of a blind, unthinking, 'culture', which alters patterns in accordance with other 'institutions' (functional analysis) or with an underlying formula (structural analysis).

I have tried in this chapter to outline an aspect of a more inclusive cultural alternation which arises from the contradictions implicit in the human situation. At one level we see a 'puritanical complex' as emerging in a religious context and as being critical of (and accompanying) the 'luxury' of Bronze Age societies, and particularly of the idea that humankind would challenge the uniqueness of the Creator God. But there is also a wider movement, epitomized in the work of Plato, that sees a more general contradiction between the reality of an object and the irreality of its representation in paint or clay, or even perhaps in words. Such a realization may well lead to the rejection of representation (the rejection of luxury has other roots) and to associated features of the 'puritanical complex', especially in wealthy merchant societies where there is some contradiction between expenditure on consumption and saving for production.

7

Towards a knowledge society

We have spoken of the circulation of information as well as of objects, but the former has further parameters. It depends on different forms of communication (linguistic, as distinct from transport) and it increasingly involves a different set of specialists: scholars rather than traders. But it has become increasingly important over the past centuries.

All societies, of course, are knowledge societies. That's what 'culture' is, partly knowledge and communication, which can be transferred and handed down because of the great human capacity of speech. It is the development of speech that has enabled *Homo sapiens* (or perhaps earlier forms) to become modern humans, to elaborate an 'extra-somatic culture' as the American anthropologist Kroeber, and others, characterized it, and to store, transfer and develop that knowledge for our offspring. As a recent view of evolution remarks: 'our own nominally civilized level of life emerged when organisms stumbled on a way of passing on intricate, unpredictable information to others around them. It did so by inventing language and effectively binding together all human organisms, past, present, and future into a single mega-organism of potentially boundless achievement.'[1] The author sees this as a continuation of biological selection; in fact, in represents a break with that mode of information transmission, so often more flexible, but involving some of the same very general 'principles', such as selection.

These features I have referred to as 'the technologies of the intellect', partly to bridge the gap between technology and the cognitive sciences. One thing that earlier anthropologists have taught us is that societies with only oral communication can be very complicated. Human society became much more so (perhaps began) with the invention of speech, giving rise, I would suggest, to thought itself, or to 'higher consciousness' in the words of the Russian psychologist Vygotsky. The so-called 'human revolution' took place with the dispersal of *Homo sapiens* from Africa some 60,000 years ago (according to DNA evidence) with a fully developed language.[2] The revolution has often been associated with France and with the appearance of cave art.[3] But cave art had a rather limited distribution in southern France and northern Spain. Anyhow, the point is that, given this technology of the intellect – that is, speech – humans developed what we call 'a culture', once it enabled us to communicate quite differently, one to another.

At first such transmission was very slow and conservative by today's standards. In the Lower and Middle Palaeolithic, human achievements had been broadly similar in various parts of the world, for example in hand-axe cultures. Take an Acheulian instrument whose form persisted over thousands of years in many parts of the globe. This was not simply 'functional' – there are many ways of killing a bison – but a cultural element was involved in the adoption and continued use of the type. The Upper Palaeolithic saw the advent of modern humans with a fully fledged language, leading to what has been called the 'human revolution'. This cultural element is more obvious when we come to its varied cave-painting, and with the simultaneous development of many flake tools of magnificent craftsmanship. Complexity clearly encourages complexity, and culture, knowledge systems, became more important as human society evolved (in a social sense). With the invention of agriculture, in the Neolithic, a greater diversity of local cultures existed, in

Africa – until recently – as in America and the Pacific; these were generally the cultures the earlier anthropologists tended to study.

From the beginning an evolution was certainly taking place in the way humans communicated, but that was relatively slow (albeit fast by genetic standards) in terms of human learning. The evolution of cultures clearly speeded up enormously with the invention of human language, the human revolution of the Upper Palaeolithic. But what is so remarkable in relation to present-day society is the extraordinary development that we have seen since the invention of 'visible speech', of writing.

Knowledge systems, then, took another leap forward with the Urban Revolution of the Bronze Age, when not only did agriculture become mechanized with the adoption of the plough, the wheel and animal traction, not only did they develop the proliferation of artisanal crafts (some connected with agriculture and others with the economic stratification that accompanied this and increased exchange), but also writing was invented in about 3000 BCE, which meant that information could be communicated over time and space, since language was now a visible object which could be despatched and preserved in quite a different manner from oral speech (as in this book). In a number of productions, but beginning with *The Domestication of the Savage Mind*,[4] I have tried to outline the changes that writing has made, in the religious life, in the polity, in the economy, and in intellectual activity generally. But here I want to concentrate on one aspect, on the speed of change. While other factors are undoubtedly involved, I would highlight the rapid increase in the rate of human development from that time, only 5,000 years ago, no time at all in terms of human history, compared with what went on in the Old and New Stone Ages. This increased rapidity seems to be mainly due to writing, which provided language with an external means for the storage of information, marked another step on the build-up to an information society, and meant that not only can we store old information but we can also add new. This is what the

The Eurasian Miracle

Bronze Age invention of writing enabled us to do: to increase enormously the speed of cultural innovation.

At least, it did and it didn't. Because in the transcendental sphere of religion, one looked back to the unchanging word of God. Religious change was not impossible but God's word was nevertheless viewed as permanent, whether in the Hebrew Bible, in the Christian testaments, or in the Muslim Qu'ran. Or even, it should be added, in the Vedic scriptures or in the Confucian classics, because it is not only monotheism or even religion that can be canonized in this way. Each instance of canonization involves a looking-back to a text which continues indefinitely to act as a guide to the present. The process is necessarily conservative. If things are to change, they do so by returning to the text and maintaining that previous generations have misinterpreted the written word.

In the arts, too, there is the phenomenon of canonization. Homer's poems were recited annually at the great festival in Athens. Shakespeare receives a similar treatment, above all at a specially dedicated theatre in his birth place, Stratford-on-Avon, but his work is performed at many other places too. However, the difference is that religious canonization is distinct from the secular variety because no alternative to God's word is possible, whereas Shakespeare's work served to stimulate that of other Elizabethan and later dramatists. Secular canonization meant artistic performance which also encouraged variation; the religious form meant the recognition of the pre-eminence of a single text, and therefore of stasis. With religious art, too, there is more confinement, anyhow as far as the topic is concerned. With secularization, we find the widening of the possible subjects – for example the abandonment of the limits placed upon medieval Christian art, more variations of content emphasizing freedom of choice and individualism – which marked post-Renaissance achievement in Europe (but which had appeared earlier in other parts of the world).

Science, in this respect, was more like art than religion, except that it was built on experience of the world in a different way. In the Abbasid (750–1258) and Buyid (944–1055) periods, the Arabs translated almost all Greek science, especially Aristotle and the works attributed to him. These were written treatises which they translated partly to get acquainted with past knowledge and partly to build up their own science, which they did especially in astronomy, mathematics and medicine. For they not only translated the Greek sciences of medicine in Galen and of geography in Ptolemy but added to them, using hospitals in Baghdad, libraries in all their capitals, observatories as at Maraghah and elsewhere, including in these translations Sanskritic works from India. On the other hand, the Muslims did not look back to Greek artistic works, such as Homer's. They had their own artistic traditions to recall, the pre-Islamic poets such as Al-Quays, whose work was often imitated. So the looking-back in this sphere was localized, while in science (in technology and in medicine) it was universal and travelled easily across cultures. In these different spheres, what literacy permitted or encouraged varied in its social importance and consequences, but, throughout, it permitted a looking-back which oral discourse could not provide, except in a much more flexible, much less certain way. One thing that writing permitted in every context was this capacity for more or less permanent storage, which was important in the arts but particularly in the sciences.

I do not want to imply that, in oral societies, there is no looking back – of course there is, but it is to a more variable tradition, to a more 'mythical' past, not to written 'history'. Let me bring out the difference by referring to a personal experience that I had in the field among the LoDagaa of northern Ghana. When I worked in west Africa over a period of forty years, I recorded various versions of the long recital known as the Bagre. First I wrote it down with a pencil and paper. It took me ten days to complete the transcription, working full-time. I also wrote down every word and I believed what the inhabitants told me, that they had 'learnt' it from an elder and that it had remained the same over time. Hence, the 'myth' could be related to other permanent aspects of the social life of the LoDagaa in an unambiguous way. Subsequently, I used a portable tape recorder, made possible by the invention of the transistor which did away with the need for wireless valves. That machine had not been previously available to anthropologists working where electricity was not available and the vast majority had just taken down one version of a long myth, which was then regarded as *the* myth of the LoDagaa (or the Nambikwara, or the Kwakiutl). But when, some years later, I recorded a further version (what I call 'the Second Bagre') with its aid, I found that this was not at all the case. Even the first (twelve) lines of the Bagre, which I called 'the invocation' and which people seemed to be able to recite 'by heart' like the Lord's Prayer, even this varied in small ways from speaker to speaker. But elsewhere it was not simply verbal changes. The first part, The White Bagre, remained roughly the same because it presented an embellished account of the actual ceremonies that were being performed, and there was a relatively fixed order in which these occurred. Even so, there was some switching of that order in the recitation, some forgetting of ritual events, although in the main the versions were reasonably similar. However, the second part of the Bagre, the Black, told of the creation not so much of the world but of human culture, the way we learned to perform various tasks like making iron, including the reproduction of humankind itself. This part of the myth was more thoughtful, more speculative, and it varied much more. There was one passage in the First Bagre – the one I recorded from dictation – where the younger one of the first two men, looking for a solution to his problems on earth, climbed up to Heaven to speak directly to God (the High God) with the help of the spider (who in Akan tales is a typical trickster) whose web formed a ladder to the skies. There he witnessed the creation of a child, and met its 'mother', with whom he, as the 'father', continually quarrelled about 'ownership'. I saw this as a central ('structural') part of the narrative but also as central to the main themes, and it played a prominent part in my analysis. When I recorded the Second Bagre,[5] my surprise was great to find no mention of this incident. There was some reference to animals flying through the air, which I might have understood as a harking back to the visit to God (who was surrounded by animals), but without a written earlier version no one would have made such a connection. Indeed, God played a relatively minor part in this Second Bagre, which gave much more emphasis to the creation of human culture by the *kontome*, the beings of the wild, denizens of the hills and the streams, and half-way between humankind and the gods. In the subsequent Third Bagre that we collected and published some years later,[6] the emphasis had shifted once again from the transcendental to the human, to the idea that 'man made himself'. In other words, intellectually there had been a complete shift of one main theme in the recitation.

With the myth changing its tone in such a radical fashion, there was no question of a single version of the Bagre being attached to LoDagaa society, even in one settlement. It was impossible to derive an interpretation of the LoDagaa based upon any one version. There was no one 'charter', in the sense of the anthropologist Malinowski. For the recitation was changing all the time, independently of other shifts but relative perhaps to varied intellectual interests. So that, under these oral conditions, a recitation was totally different from the largely fixed text associated with written cultures. The myths of oral societies apparently changed constantly and that had to do, *inter alia*, with the type of storage available. In societies with writing one could learn a fixed text, as with those members of any of the Abrahamistic religions who tried to memorize the complete holy book, in a kind of homage to God, even though writing rendered this kind of memorization unnecessary. In oral conditions, however, a person could not memorize the Bagre in the same way. You heard others recite it but, when your turn came to do so, no matter whether you tried to repeat exactly what others had said (and in a long oral recitation of this kind, that was virtually impossible), you had to continue to speak. What you didn't recall, you had to make up. The public recitation demanded that gaps be filled, not left to be completed later. Consequently, as distinct from written rituals, each version was different, sometimes significantly so. As I have remarked, this was not simply a matter of small verbal changes; sometimes the very 'structure' of the recitation differed (and I use that word advisedly). That is to say, there could be (and was) a switch from a transcendental explanation of the origins of culture to a human one, or a shift from the role of the High God to that of intermediaries such as the beings of the wild (known to English speakers as the fairies).

The conclusion I want to bring out is this. In an oral society, the process of looking back is very different from that in a literate one. An oral society is in a certain sense more 'creative'; the myth is never the same, although it may have elements in common. Whereas, with writing, we have a firm base in a 'text', one that cannot be changed because it is God's word, religious, transcendental. Or that of a canonical writer. But in other spheres of activity we look back in a different way, to build upon what has been written, whether in the arts where change is of a more or less circular kind, or in science and technology where one explanation often improves upon the earlier, and constructs upon that. And in that context, it is not simply writing that counts but other changes or differences in the means of communication that may lead to a more accurate or more rapid circulation of information. And this is where printing, by wood blocks or by the press, by the hand, steam-driven or rotary press, by the various forms of computer, comes in. These technologies too can circulate useful information more quickly and more widely, but they can also circulate other messages of quite a different order in the same way.

This invention of writing led to the introduction of schools where people could learn to read and write, segregated from the world in special establishments. Schools led to universities where teachers, bureaucrats and priests could be trained. Priests because, while writing was used for secular purposes such as trade (especially in Mesopotamia), it also led to the recording of religious ideas and to the production of Scriptures, of canonical texts (especially in the Abrahamistic religions). Whereas the former (secular uses) were constantly changing, the latter were fixed because they represented the word of God or of one of his prestigious messengers; therefore they had to remain fixed and certain. This happened not only with the monotheistic religions but also with polytheistic Hinduism (in the Rgvedas) and with creeds like Buddhism (where the canon was printed) and even with ideologies like Confucianism in China, although in this latter case teachings were oriented not towards the supernatural but towards humankind.

Faith versus reason

Literate societies tended to develop religious systems which took charge of education (as a way of reproducing themselves) and so restricted the flow of information to what was needed to establish their view of the world. This happened with the Abrahamistic religions, namely Judaism, Christianity and Islam. All three religions tended initially to adopt a view that enquiry was unnecessary because God had laid down the way things were, and therefore human investigation in these matters was not worthwhile. God had already said all there was to say. This was the opinion of St Augustine. It was apparent in the remarks of the Caliph Umar, the Islamic conqueror of Cairo, before the remnants of the great Greek library of Alexandria. It was clear in Judaic education which, as with the other religions of the Abrahamistic faith, was concerned more with memorizing what had already been written, than with producing the new and investigating how the world was.

But there was always a problem. Teach somebody to read and write, and they can study the Scriptures. That was the aim of schools in eighteenth-century France, as the historians Furet and Ozouf have shown,[7] and as the autobiography of the Jewish philosopher Maimon demonstrates for early nineteenth-century Poland. It was, after all, the reason that all these religions, Protestant as well as Catholic, set up schools, for religious purposes, though traders also had their interests in learning to read and write for commercial purposes. So too did administrators (in the west, often clerics). But teach someone to read and it can never stop there; it is also to place in their hands a revolutionary instrument of the knowledge society, which may stimulate some to look at and even compose other writings, those of philosophers as well as those of theologians, at other paths of history, for not all were followers of the Book, of the Holy Scriptures. There were, after all, the Greek writers who did not adhere to a hegemonic religion. Among them, thinking was freer, more 'pagan', polytheistic; Homer, though ubiquitous and ritualized, did not restrict knowledge in the same way. Nor did Confucianism.

Writing and the accumulation of information

So one of the greatest steps towards a knowledge society came with the invention of writing. There are certain scholars, like the philosopher Derrida, who see 'writing' as embedded in the memory traces of speech even in purely oral societies. This position depends upon a metaphorical usage in that it disregards, disrespects, history. In any view of the Bronze Age, its invention of the first writing systems in Mesopotamia and Egypt (about 3000 BCE), and subsequently in India in the Indus Valley and in China in the Yellow River Valley (approximately 1500 BCE), and not forgetting Central America (a very distinct situation), revolutionized human society. Let us set aside for the moment the possible stimuli for the invention of the written word – mercantile developments perhaps in Mesopotamia,[8] royal divination in China,[9] religion possibly in Egypt, politics elsewhere – for it is the consequences (or implications) that matter. In Mesopotamia, for example, there were considerable advances in social organization, with the administration of the ruler being soon complicated by the recording of decisions and the archiving of correspondence; and in learning, too. There were advances in mathematics and the computation of surface areas (for taxation purposes), as well as the calculation of space (for the same ends) and of time (for calendrical purposes). But there was also literature in the form of the story of Enlil, of poetry and, in a sense, of painting too, though that too existed beforehand (as had verse and some telling of myths). Literacy, in the sense of an ability to read and write, led in turn to the extraordinary success of Greece (and Rome), to the whole array of achievements of classical society which were down not so much to the Greek genius as to the increased circulation of writing in an alphabetic script among the elite, as well as the greater reflexivity that it imposes upon the use of language.

The alphabetic script was invented in Greece, or rather in Phoenicia in all its essentials, except that Phoenician script did not have letter signs for vowels. Europeans have made much of this difference. But it is not as important as many, trying to build up the European advantage in matters of communication, have believed. The Semitic scripts used diacriticals to indicate vowels and have produced long and interesting work using this script – on which all Indian versions are based – including the Bible itself among their achievements. Moreover, it is obvious that even 'earlier' scripts, such as the logographic one used in China, could produce a highly complex civilization, which in this case was run by literati for over 2,000 years; these men were trained to read the classics in a society that, as the sinologist Joseph Needham has shown, was scientifically in advance of the west at least until the Renaissance. And science and technology were at least partly a matter of circulating information in writing. It was writing indeed that, after the Bronze Age, assisted humanity in taking such a decisive step towards 'modernity' and saw the accumulation of knowledge in Mesopotamia, Egypt, in Greece and Rome, in India and China. From then on, civilization, culture, proceeded by leaps and bounds; innovations came and were adopted in a much faster way.

The presence of writing was one major factor that increased the flow of information and made for a 'knowledge society'. I have hinted that the script was another, it being widely assumed that the alphabet was more democratic and more alphabetic than the logographic characters of China. As far as learning was concerned, the alphabet was as easy as ABC and therefore potentially all could learn, but in China one does not need to learn a whole system to understand an inscription or a banner; we learn using sign by wordsign. And in the period before the Renaissance, China appears to have had a higher rate of literacy, of people who could read and write (but what?) than any other society.

Chinese literacy warrants a further comment. As a logographic script, the equivalent of our mathematical notation, it could represent the diversity of languages within the borders of China, and this served to hold this immense and complex country together and hence to provide a unified 'market' for both commercial and intellectual goods. The USA has done the same by insisting upon a single language, English, and thus demoting all others. The EU has tried to establish a single market and retain the languages of all the participants (which it could do more easily if it had Esperanto in addition). China, at less cultural cost than the first and with greater efficiency than the latter, pursued a different course, a single script for all languages. It could be argued that the EU (and Switzerland) might consider whether a phonetic script was best adapted to a multilingual community, or whether they might consider the Chinese alternative, despite Lenin's pronouncement that alphabetization was the revolution of the east. Though it may be for the keyboard.

What was as important as – or more important than – script, in advancing a knowledge society, was the material on which you write, whether this was clay tablets, bamboo strips, wooden plaques, silk, parchment or paper.[10] The invention of paper in China about the second century BCE meant you had a cheap and universally available medium for communicating information with others (or with yourself for that matter). Whereas, in Europe, with animal skins (parchment), you had to kill a dozen sheep to produce the material for a book. That difference meant that in China (and the Islamic Near East after the battle of Talas), you had some large libraries – the imperial library in China in 978 CE consisted of 80,000 books, the library of al-Hakam in Cordoba in the tenth century had 400,000 'books' – whereas the largest library in northern Europe at that time, at the monastery of St Gall in Switzerland, had some 800 volumes. The difference is staggering and results from the fact that Europe did not have paper until its manufacture came to Italy from the Muslim world in the twelfth century (in England, not till some centuries later).

The mechanization of writing

The amount of information and its availability to the population was of course massively increased in the west by the invention of printing by movable type and with a unique use of the printing press, attributed to the German Gutenberg, in the middle of the fifteenth century. Not immediately, but gradually, books became cheaper for all. Previously in a scriptoria it might take a man six months to copy by hand a sizeable manuscript. This changed at once with the introduction of print and the press.

But the west was not the first to mechanize writing. The Chinese had done it long before with woodblock printing, in which you carved the script on a piece of wood. Interestingly, in expert hands, this did not take significantly longer than setting up a page of type, which the Chinese had also invented (that is, moveable type, also using an alphabetic script, though not a press). While printing possibly did not have the revolutionary effect that it had in the west, it was certainly important in permitting the increased flow of information during the Song period in China (around the tenth century), which has been spoken of as a Renaissance, so important was it for knowledge in that country. Libraries, both public and private, increased significantly in numbers and in size, as did the incidence of schooling and of publications. There can be no doubt that the great achievements of science in China before the Italian Renaissance were significantly due to the rapidity of information flow throughout this enormous country, which in an important way was held together by writing in a logographic script. This script enabled Cantonese to communicate with Mandarin speakers or with Vietnamese, and so to have a much larger knowledge society, without knowing those languages.

The Chinese developed the printed word, albeit using woodblock printing. But, unlike paper, they never transmitted this technique to Islam, basically for religious reasons. In Islam, you could not print the name of God, or indeed the language of his book; consequently, Islam fell behind in the move towards a knowledge society, in which the use of paper had made it so advanced at an earlier period. So, until relatively recently, one did not find newspapers in Islamic countries, nor even novels or textbooks, which more or less depend on the printed word, except for those written in long-hand.

The modern equivalents of printing which give access to large amounts of information are, of course, the computer and the internet. Here the advantage was obviously with those who invented these technologies, the computer in Anglo-American circles (initially stimulated by the need to analyse codes), the internet in the US military, the software by Microsoft and others. The result has certainly been to democratize information. We have seen it as creating the knowledge society. But all human societies have been concerned with the flow of information in its various ways, and that is in no sense a permanent advantage of the west. Writing, paper, print, all came to us from other societies which had an advantage in communication until the Renaissance, perhaps even until the nineteenth century with the coming of steam-driven, industrialized, printing presses. But that temporary advantage is now leaving us. China and India (perhaps Islam next) are catching up; Europe is off-loading many tasks connected with knowledge to India (by outsourcing) and, for the manufacture of computers, to China and east Asia. These techniques are no longer confined to the west and we increasingly have to see the world as belonging to a single knowledge society based upon the electronic transfer of information, a more rapid globalization than has taken place with writing, or paper, or print.

Knowledge systems have clearly played an important part in European history since the Renaissance and have therefore played a prominent role in the 'triumph of capitalism'. But it is by placing their role in a historical context that one can properly evaluate what has happened, for, ever since the Italian Renaissance with its role in modernization, in globalization, we are not alone, but part of a Eurasian network.

8

The temporary advantage in alternation of the post-Renaissance west

I have argued that there appears to be little unique in some of the conditions for the undoubted advantage that Europe enjoyed in the nineteenth century. The problem with most accounts of the situation in the past, and specifically the one that has emerged in the present day, is that they rely on essentialist premises and are therefore ethnocentric and teleological in relation to recent European achievements. These achievements were undoubtedly important, but they do not acknowledge alternation between east and west; that is to say, they need to start from a rough parallel in the development of art and arts in the widest sense, and, with regard to the sciences and technology, they must allow for a pattern in which first one civilization, then another, takes the lead.

In this discussion, I have been trying to modify the difference that many in the west have drawn between European and Asian societies, seeing them not as incompatible or incomparable, nor as taking different paths of development, as Marx, Weber and many others have supposed, but as two areas taking roughly parallel routes. This parallelism is well illustrated in Needham's magnificent series,[1] in Ledderose's discussion of the division of labour in the Chinese porcelain industry,[2] in the note by Elvin that certain Italian textile machinery (for reeling thread mechanically) was first developed in China,[3] in the immense importance of paper and printing (albeit by woodblocks) for the communication, reading and development of information, in China's invention of gunpowder too, as Francis Bacon pointed out – in all these ways China preceded the west. Until the end of the eighteenth century it was the largest exporting nation in the world (no doubt with India coming not far behind). So when we now see China and India making such an important contribution to the world economy, this is nothing new, but a revival of the past, an alternation. What is surprising is that until recently most European historians and other scholars did not recognize the achievements of Asiatic societies before the so-called 'Industrial Revolution' but characterized that region in quite other terms, as 'primitive', as 'backward', as 'Oriental'. That was essentially because they adopted an inappropriate unilineal 'evolutionary' schema of development which ran from hunting and gathering economies through to the industrialization of nineteenth-century Britain in a direct line, with post-Bronze Age Asia going off on a tangent of the so-called 'Asiatic mode of production', or Asiatic exceptionalism, to try to account for the absence of modernization, of industrialization, of capitalism, in that part of the world over the last few centuries.

My own approach began with the understanding that both parts of the landmass of Europe and Asia had experienced the Bronze Age, that is, the search for metals, the elaboration of many crafts, the development of the plough and of animal traction (adding to human energy), the coming of the wheel and then of writing. It was this change in the mode of communication that struck me first. With my collaborator, Ian Watt, I looked at the difference alphabetic writing had made in earlier Greece, in antiquity, and emphasized its role in encouraging an easy mode of written communication which was preferred as an explanation for the achievements of that society to one in terms of discussions of the Greek 'genius', Hellenic spirit or Attic mentality generally. However, ours was a distinctly European account, trying to account for the achievement of antiquity and the course of its voyage to the Renaissance, and thence to modernity. What we omitted was properly to consider the fact that the holy book of Europe had been written without the benefit of the Greek (or even Phoenician) alphabet, but in a Semitic language on the Asian shore. Of course, this location did not matter very much to those Protestants who thought of Palestine as part of Europe[4] but it led me to widen the alphabetic thesis to include Semitic and other Middle Eastern literatures which were not written in the same way. And, looking beyond the Near East, it became necessary to consider other forms of writing and the contributions the societies employing them had made to 'civilization', to the culture of cities, especially the Chinese whose script, following the notions of many Europeans, we had seen as difficult, elitist and non-democratic. But its use seems to have been much wider than we supposed,[5] partly because one could learn Chinese icon by icon without having to break a phonetic code. The concept of a literate person was consequently much looser. Second, as we have seen, a non-phonetic logographic script had the extraordinary potential of serving for all the many languages of China and keeping a large polity together. In any case, we certainly made a mistake in downplaying the potentiality of cultural achievement with a Chinese-type script which, as a form of writing, had so many other things to recommend it.

All these considerations spoke in favour of the compatibility of eastern and western cultures, rather than the built-in supremacy of the west. Yet there was something to be said in favour of European achievement. What the Greeks accomplished was remarkable by any standard (including Alexander's conquests), and on the literacy level one only has to look at the range of work in the standard classical Loeb library to appreciate the point. But what was an error in this discussion was not simply the neglect of other forms of writing and their many achievements, but the idea that the supremacy of the west was established in antiquity and proceeded from that point in a sequence of antiquity, feudalism, capitalism. This progression did not allow for alternation between the west and the east, nor for the changes in achievements within these cultures.

This latter alternation can be seen quite clearly in Europe after antiquity. As Needham explains for the study of botany, the Chinese and Europeans were more or less at level pegging in terms of the numbers of species identified (in writing) at the time of Aristotle's pupil Theophrastus, about the fourth century BCE. After that, in the west, there was a rapid decline in knowledge during the feudal period, whereas China proceeded slowly until, at the time of the Renaissance, the west suddenly caught up and drew ahead in a movement which I have recently examined comparatively.[6] This earlier growth and relapse in Europe was followed by a burst leading to the present position of western supremacy, a growth which was related to the use of water power, of iron and coal, the economy, the revival of secular learning, and development of the printing press. The situation applied to many other fields. The point is that, whereas Europe may have had an advantage over the east in classical times (or were the civilizations already at level pegging?), in the feudal period the west underwent what has been called 'a catastrophic regression' in various ways, only picking up again in the Renaissance of the twelfth century and, more especially, in the later Italian Renaissance. At that time Europe certainly did begin to take a lead, which it consolidated with the Industrial Revolution, some of the origins of which lay in the east. Given this alternation, one must discard essentialist explanations of the kind that Europe took up, explanations in terms of 'spirit', 'mentality', even culture (in one interpretation of that elusive concept); all these had to be set aside. We should therefore not look back to essentialist explanations of 'capitalism' or 'modernization' as many sociologists and historians, including the American historian David Landes in a widely read book, have done.[7] The reason for China's so-called 'backwardness' in the nineteenth century did not need to refer to any deep-seated cultural factors, but was the result of an alternation. For example, after the Tang, the Song dynasty became more secular, more Confucian (or rather Neo-

Confucian) and experienced a revolution in the arts and in the sciences, a period which had a certain flavour of Renaissance about it since it involved a looking-back and a going-forward along a wide front. I argue that all cultures with writing had periods when they looked back, sometimes in a religious way – leading generally to stasis – and sometimes in a more secular manner – often resulting in invention. You had forward-looking periods in Maurya and Gupta India, as well as in Islam during Abbasid times and, later, in Andalusia. Another looking-back occurred in the Italian Renaissance, but there was one vital difference: the alternation then apparently ceased and you got a more permanent transformation, the kind of continuous, self-sustaining growth that (according to Rostow) has been regarded as typical of a 'capitalist' economy.[8] Whereas in Islam and in India, and in a more secular way even in China, one finds a period of liberalization of this kind followed by a resurgence of beliefs in a transcendental universe, in Renaissance Europe the demand for more secular explanations ('scientific', we might call them) remained, and knowledge about the world continued to expand.

What gave rise to this situation? Hardly the Protestant ethic since, while less successful movements of reform, such as the Lollards, appeared earlier, the Protestants did not really make a mark until the sixteenth century. Again 'capitalism' could hardly be responsible, as it seems to have existed as mercantile capitalism much earlier, and as financial capitalism (to use Braudel's distinction) only later.

My own account is as follows. A deliberate looking-back was experienced in the Italian Renaissance, a looking-back that, in its broad dimensions, was intrinsic to literacy, a process which characterized all written cultures in Eurasia – Christianity, Islam, India and China, to name but the major ones. It is a feature of all those that have a written religion which necessarily involves looking back to the Book, to the holy word of God (or of his mouthpiece), especially in monotheistic creeds which are in many ways hegemonic. But, from time to time, such a looking-back is to a less demanding ideology that gives more space to the secular, and this, to my mind, is what happened with the return to classical society in Renaissance Europe and to Confucianism in Song China, jumping over the hegemony of Christianity in one case and of Buddhism in the other. Of course, such internal alternation may occur under other circumstances, as in India, where the secular vision of the non-transcendental Lokayata held a more permanent place in the total picture, and that universe was not only 'spiritual' as the French anthropologist Louis Dumont, and others, have maintained. But alternation was the rule, rather than continuous 'growth' towards one end.

The transcendental re-asserted itself, especially with a dominant 'church' which claimed a monopoly on all accounts of both this world and the next. In the case of Christianity, Islam and Buddhism, that church had far-reaching tentacles that established schools to train individuals to read the scripture, that accumulated land, buildings (including hospitals, markets and places of worship), which ensured their hegemony and their continuity over time (as distinct from the more ephemeral creeds of oral cultures). These religions asserted their dominance, as did the Vedic ones whose Brahman caste controlled education, in much the same way that priestly groups did in Europe, and the *ulama* in Islam, the monks in Buddhism and even the literati in 'secular' Confucianism. What was different about the Italian Renaissance in Europe was that the switch to a more secular attitude became institutionalized, became a permanent and not a transitional feature of the intellectual landscape. This was essentially because education and learning finally got taken out of the hands of the church (mainly in the interests of the growing bourgeoisie) and so enquiry (and hence 'science') was freer. It got taken out of transcendental hands partly by looking back to a 'pagan' society: Greece or Rome in the case of the Italian Renaissance and, to a less complete extent, in the Abbasid period of Islam; to Confucianism in the case of the Song. And this shift was institutionalized, rendered more stable, in the Italian Renaissance by the rise of learning in the more 'secular' universities of Europe. This was not the beginning of the rise of higher education, because that existed beforehand, usually for religious purposes, and it was closely tied to the priesthood and to transcendental religion (except under Confucian China). This was particularly the case with the madrasas of the Islamic world, whose establishment was part of a Sunni attempt to re-establish 'orthodoxy' and to concentrate on religious education, excluding what they called 'foreign sciences'. The madrasas have sometimes been seen as the model for western universities – the Al Azhar of Cairo being called the 'Sorbonne of Islam' – but in fact most 'science' fell outside their remit, as of course did secular thinking more widely. What distinguished the institutions of higher learning in the west from those of Islam or Buddhism, but less so from those in China, was the long-term institutionalization of secular (non-religious) learning. This was not immediately so, for most of the earlier European universities, such as that at Paris, were directed to the training of priests and religiously oriented administrators. But not all. Bologna had a secular foundation in a town that was not ruled by the Papacy and was strongly connected with the revival of trade in northern Italy, especially in the Mediterranean with Byzantium and the east. It was Ghibelline rather than Guelf, under the auspice of the Emperor rather than the Pope. This gave that city, and its offshoot at Padua, a greater independence to encourage other subjects and approaches, as in the teaching of Roman, as distinct from ecclesiastical, law. Such independence was partly due to the role played by the economy in the whole effort of the Italian Renaissance, by the recovery of trade and manufacture, which included the production of paper (from China), the early use of water-driven machinery – including the acquisition from Lucca and eventually (probably) from China of the mechanization of the reeling of thread for the weaving of textiles, first silk, then cotton, in the so-called 'Industrial Revolution'.

The relative independence of the north Italian cities and their universities, especially Bologna and Venice, was made possible principally by the rebirth of commercial activity. Venice experienced the revival of trade in the Mediterranean and the Near East; Bologna supplied some of the exports transported down the River Po; Florence played its part. Trade and manufacture, the activities of the bourgeoisie, were essential to this Renaissance, as to many others. It was the production of commodities for exchange that gave the community much of the wealth needed for promoting art, literature and learning in the way that it did. Not that this was the only backing a Renaissance required. Indeed, Iraq and Persia were apparently not very prosperous under what has been called the Buyid Renaissance, but this was most unusual; in many spheres, wealth is employed to support the going-forward, as Jardine has emphasized for the Italian Renaissance.

But prosperity is only one of the supports. Another feature is the one we have mentioned in respect of all literate societies: a looking-back to an earlier state of affairs. When that means looking back to an earlier regime that was less hegemonic, less transcendental, the results could be spectacular, as was the case in Italy – looking beyond Catholicism – or in the Song – looking beyond Buddhism. In comparison with the pre-existing states of affairs, this involved a secularization: what Weber called 'a demystification' of belief. This had to do not so much with the Protestant ethic, as he had claimed, since it also occurred in Catholic circles – as, of course, did capitalism – but came from looking back to a 'pagan' society, as well as drawing on a critical aspect of belief, or even disbelief, that seems a general feature of human life,[9] though often subterranaean. The emergence of this strand was not unusual in written cultures, nor indeed even in oral ones, but in the west it ceased to be only an alternative approach and became a permanent – and in some respects a dominant – feature, largely due to its incorporation in institutions of higher learning. These were not the first universities, as I have remarked; there were many in India, under mainly Buddhist, but also Jain and Hindu, influence. But, perhaps barring China, they were the first to institutionalize secular knowledge, at least since antiquity. Why they did so is not easy to say because many were devoted to training those priests and ecclesiastically oriented administrators. This was the case not only in Paris, but in early Oxford and Cambridge as well, not to mention the universities in the Papal states. For even secular universities were strongly influenced by the dominant religion, which led in part to the importance of Faculties of Theology.[10] And the discussion of many scientific topics was affected by the transcendental beliefs of others. Certainly in Europe the great civic universities, founded by rich bourgeois families, were among the first to institutionalize secular learning on a permanent basis. The bulk of western universities did secularize their curriculum in important ways so that teaching and research in the sciences and in the humanities grew and were eventually strengthened, and the religious component became of less and less importance, that of secular learning more and more so.

Why did this institutionalization of the secular happen in the west rather than the east? Not because of the ethics of Protestantism. The tendency had been there before, most markedly since the increase in trade in the later Middle Ages.[11] For education was necessary not simply for churchmen and for administrators but also for merchants, who had views on how their children should be educated and, with their increasing prestige, could – if not programme – at least influence the curriculum of schools and universities. The historian Nicholas' account of late medieval education in Holland emphasizes the role merchants had come to play in education. As the economy expanded, so too did their role, which required both literacy and numeracy. The involvement of the merchants was also a strong feature of the Grammar Schools of the Elizabethan period. Take the example of my own school at St Albans, reputedly started as an adjunct to the Abbey in 908. Despite the Elizabethan charter, which guaranteed it a proportion of the wine duty, it remained in the Lady Chapel of the Abbey church until the middle of the nineteenth century, when a certain silk manufacturer in the town (Woollams) arranged for the purchase of the old Abbey gateway for it. Later, in 1908, the school moved to its first purpose-made buildings nearby. But it was attended by the sons of merchants (in former days it had probably provided the first English Pope, Nicholas Breakspeare), which indeed is what the Elizabethan Foundation was expressly for. The merchants were not against a religious education for their sons, but they wanted that kept in its place. They would have favoured the humanist approach.

It was the same at the universities. They soon found themselves overproducing clerical personnel. They increasingly produced secular administrators like Sir Thomas More, who escaped the vigilance of his church, and poets and playwrights too when those activities became acceptable once again; and there were, of course, schoolteachers for the increasing range of Grammar Schools, who were only partly men of the cloth.

It is not that commerce was more important in the west than in the east before the nineteenth century, even though the influence of iron machinery and steam power greatly increased production in the eighteenth. Even well before that time, as the historian and geographer Wrigley has pointed out, Europe was well placed to export iron, which it did when it came to the Industrial Revolution, because of its underground deposits of iron and coal, and of the knowledge and expertise in their exploitation. The production of iron in the west seems to have fallen back since the Roman period when enormous amounts were required – by, among others, the military – but iron ore was widely processed in medieval bloomeries. Its mass production was partly a matter of demand, especially in the western agricultural areas of Flanders and England, and it was radically increased with the development of the blast furnace. First, the bellows and hammers in the traditional smelting concerns were adapted to the use of water power. Then, in the late Middle Ages, came the bloomery producing a high-carbon iron which was suitable for casting. Finally, the problem of quantity was addressed by the use of the blast furnace after the fifteenth century, a high shaft furnace where ore and carbon were suitably mixed to form iron carbide, which had a lower melting point for producing cast iron, which then had to be refined to make wrought iron. It is uncertain where this first developed but southern Flanders is said to be the most likely place. This 'Walloon' process was brought to England at the end of the fifteenth century[12] at Newbridge, Sussex, in 1496, an invention that overlapped with the development of water power.[13] Significantly, according to Needham,[14] the Chinese had been 'great masters of the art of iron-casting ever since the 1st century', while the blast furnace is dated to the third century BCE.[15] All this metal was very important in providing material for exports, including of machinery, when it came to the Industrial Revolution.

However, merchant activity became somewhat more independent than earlier and was able to offer a more secular education at an early stage. Humanism, merchants and technology obviously played their part in this endeavour, the schools aiming for a curriculum that was not limited to the religious. And this trend was no longer subject to the alternation that had marked previous renascences, but was fixed because such thinking was institutionalized in schools and universities. It was able to pursue its own course towards modernization, with one generation building on the work of another without the kind of reversion to the dominance of the church that occurred elsewhere. Except in China, where the move in the forward direction was, as Needham has pointed out, slower but more regular, without the spectacular advance of what he tendentiously calls 'modern' science but making progress in that direction and acquiring techniques from the west, just as the west had earlier acquired them from the east. We have spoken of internal alternation between the religious and the secular. There was also the external alternation of societal prominence which we are all experiencing today. Alternation can occur at a societal or regional level, as we have discussed regarding east and west, with the great shift to the west coming between the Renaissance and the nineteenth century; previously there had been a movement in the other direction at the end of the Roman period. But the switch may be partial, involving specific realms – such as the agricultural or iron production – and may involve different measures. The important point is to abandon the notion of perpetual supremacy of one or the other and to adopt a more flexible approach that takes account of past and present realities.

History does not flow in quite the lines that much social evolutionary theory requires. There has been an oscillation between one society and another, partly because the process of catching up, however it occurs, is always stimulating, so that they who were behind at one moment may well be ahead at the next. Neither the west nor the east was unique in this sense. They were intercommunicating systems, one of whom had an advantage, then another. History did not and does not move in the straight lines that essentialist accounts assume.

9

Alternation in Eurasia

To summarize the argument, I have tried to propose a contrast to the common, western, idea of the permanent, or even long-term, dominance or superiority of Europe in its trajectory to modernization or capitalism. This idea is embodied in the notion that the modern world has evolved out of antiquity, feudalism and capitalism, a line of development which was not open to the Orient. I have argued that this is a totally mistaken view of the east. This has to be seen as entering into Bronze Age culture from the Ancient Near East at roughly the same period, starting 3000 BCE, which represented the beginning of Eurasian 'civilization'. This developed equally both in the east and in the west, giving rise to written cultures in the Near East, in India, in China, in Greece and then in Rome. None of these societies had a privileged route to 'modernity', much less to 'capitalism'. They developed from that time in vaguely parallel ways, not diverging into Asiatic and European modes, but, as Wolf has suggested,[1] in a 'tributary mode', which may have been somewhat more authoritarian and centralized in the east than in the west. Otherwise, there is no case for a distinct phase called 'antiquity' which was confined to the west, nor yet for a feudalism, similarly limited. Of course, the subsequent outcomes differed, then as now, but not to the extent implied in many evolutionary schemes, as well as in common parlance in which it is only the west that found modernization possible, unless the others did so by diffusion from a more advanced centre. And I am thinking not only of the fixed schemes proposed by Marx but of a much wider array, embodied in this historical view of the west which dictated that others were structurally incapable (through 'mentality'?) of making the necessary leap forward, of conquering the world physically, economically and culturally.

But the modern world was not simply a question of diffusion, of exporting 'capitalism'. Japan did not just accept what the Americans and Europeans had brought. At first, they appeared (from the western viewpoint) to be producing cheap metal toys less expensively than elsewhere, with a badly paid workforce. But this view did not persist over the longer term. For the country also produced sturdy battleships to defeat the Russians, and excellently constructed cameras that conquered the world – all this was preceded not only by a process of imitation but by building on a long tradition of local manufacture and knowledge. Much social history made an exception for the Japanese in their move towards modernity. They could engage in this because they had a mentality, a social structure ('bilateral' kinship), a history (feudalism, unlike China) which enabled them to take a different direction from the rest of the east.

Adequate as this may have appeared in order to explain the great advance made by Japan, it was soon shown to be incorrect. First, the countries of south-east Asia (the Little Tigers, especially Korea and Malaysia) made their own very strong contribution to modernization, contrary to the theory that singled out Japan. Then the giants of the east started to show their strength: China in manufacturing and in intellectual output, in space technology and in international events; India in the universities and in information technology. On a theoretical level, these nations were excluded from the process of modernization, for Japan alone (because of 'feudalism') was considered to be in line for the development of capitalism. Now these others have all joined in the move to 'modernity', putting on one side the arguments that saw Japan as an eastern branch of Europe, as well as the many analyses that drew attention to the differences of that country from China and India. Much of this 'essentialist' discussion has turned out to be misplaced. The major countries of the east were much more alike than these theories required, much more like the European too in the broad lines of their development.

These subsequent events – the growth of Chinese manufactures, the re-assumption of the country's earlier position as a great exporting power, its recent adventures in space, its production of an electric car (with the commercial research efforts that this required) – all this should make us rethink not only its place in contemporary society but its place in world history leading up to this moment. How could the west have got it so wrong? But the alternative account was very convincing and, in the nineteenth and twentieth centuries, very persuasive. It included the notions that Europe, exclusively, went back to the achievements of antiquity, of Greece and Rome, and that this gave way in turn to an exclusive feudalism, and then to an exclusive Renaissance that saw the rebirth of part, at least, of that antiquity in some new social formation: that of 'capitalism'. But, in fact, that capitalism was much more widely distributed, as Braudel recognized. 'Sprouts of capitalism' were discovered in China, even by Marxist authors, so that nothing remained singular in the west, except possibly 'finance capitalism', in Braudel's phrase; nor as I have suggested elsewhere was there anything absolutely unique, neither in the trajectory from antiquity to feudalism, nor in the concept of the Renaissance.[2] These were events arising out of a common history of the development of 'civilization' from the Bronze Age to the present day. Since that time we have a measure of level-pegging, as well as times when one society gained an advantage over the others, but this was only a temporary state of affairs since this position was characterized by the existence of alternation between the major societies – first one then another emerging as leaders.

One of the main factors I see as contributing to the pre-eminence of Europe since the Renaissance is that we no longer have quite the same 'internal' alternation between dominance of a transcendental view of the world and dominance of a more secular outlook that encourages a scientific approach to the universe. I have suggested elsewhere that, in Islam and in Hinduism, we had an internal alternation between the latter two. Until, that is, when we came to the Renaissance, when a tradition of secular enquiry was institutionalized in the universities, especially in the urban centres of northern Italy. From that time on, higher education became increasingly dominated by the secular and increasingly devoted to understanding the world outside the framework of the world religions. Previously, these had taken charge of not only primary education, when it was involved in training the younger generation to read the Book, but in higher education which was devoted to the training of priests and of ecclesiastical administrators. Technology was usually neutral as far as transcendental beliefs were concerned, which is not to deny that there were devils in Ethiopian watermills, and in Islam printing was not possible. While technology was usually free, there can be little doubt that minds were set at liberty not only by the Renaissance but by the process of secularization that preceded it. Under such influences, the economy opened up. Venice traded with the infidel Turk and partly broke away from the influence of Rome. This encouraged the trade in metals which was one of the foremost elements in the economy. Techniques improved; machinery was developed, iron became a common material, and more coal was mined to smelt it. Productivity increased. As another example shows, the recent rise in agricultural production in Africa with the introduction of cheap iron tools (hoe blades, machetes) from Europe was remarkable. Not until iron and coal were available on this scale did iron technology (which already existed in Africa) really make a great impression on local agriculture.

For external alternation between the major societies of the Eurasian landmass is an outcome of the many routes, for traders, for migration and for war, that have threaded through both parts. It is an aspect of the communication between cultures which means that first one flourished, then another, since one fertilized the other. This is particularly clear after the Bronze Age when the great advances in the 'culture of cities' that had been created in Mesopotamia and Egypt at around 3000 BCE spread eastwards to India and China and westwards to Greece and Rome. Mesopotamia's achievements in mathematics were taken up and elaborated in the east in India and China, in the west by Greece. In all this, there was a certain equality, but often at radically different times, so that in a certain period one culture led the way, to be followed by the rest. These differences, built on a common basis, involved differences in resources, including metals and agricultural products – like tea in China – as well as in manufactured products such as paper and gunpowder, together with information of other kinds – all items which formed part of the exchange economy, involving the use of the generalized means of exchange, money. This exchange was a dynamic process with one party largely in receipt at one moment, but the other eventually taking the lead, not being permanently behindhand. There was thus a kind of alternation in the economy, as well as in knowledge systems, not necessarily all coinciding but tending to do so, since so much depended upon the former. It is just such an alternation we are experiencing today, with China and India beginning to dominate the manufacturing economy and the search for new materials, and beginning too to influence the educational process and the conquest of space. There is no longer a single dominant power, but one that has to contend with the others, with alternatives.

I am using this concept of 'alternation' in opposition to the kind of supremacy that so many western commentators see as marking the west. If we phrase it in Marxist terms, the Asiatic mode of production could not lead to modernization, which could occur only under capitalism, preceded by feudalism. This line of argument tended to exclude China from the pathway to modernization, unless assisted by the

Communist parties of Europe (as Moscow proposed), or unless we posit a stage of feudalism (as some scholars have done, while, as we have seen, yet others have discovered 'sprouts of capitalism') – all attempts to open up China to the possibility of modernization. But China did not need this. It was never frozen in the way that western-oriented evolutionary theory suggested. The answer was to understand the comparability, over time, of the major Bronze Age societies, which continued in later ages. The comparability continued, but at times one society inevitably drew ahead of another in the development of increasingly complex systems, especially because the advent of writing had encouraged the heightened tempo of cultural change. But any such advantage was only temporary, mainly due to the fact that these cultures were continuously communicating, exchanging one product against another, or against abstract media of exchange. So we get not permanent supremacy but the alternation of cultures, not in every aspect but in many, and especially in science and technology.

We can see this alternation in process today, in Japan, in China, in India, in south-east Asia. Nor is this simply a matter of the theft of techniques of capitalism from the west. In the first place, the west had earlier adopted a number of techniques from the east and, until the end of the eighteenth century, China, not the west, had been the greatest exporting power. So its present position does not represent a new situation born of having adopted western 'capitalism' but one of reclaiming a position, with regard to manufacturing (of porcelain, silk, bronze, lacquer and paper), which it had held well before. There had been an alternation in Eurasian society, with the various exports stimulating competitive production (as at Meissen, Delft, the Potteries and elsewhere). The roots of the Industrial Revolution lay in the development of techniques that had been borrowed over the Eurasian landmass, transmitted by the constant trading back and forth, so that the birth of 'capitalism' occurred in the east and the west and was but one part of an alternation. Capitalism in a general sense, as Braudel suggests, was not the invention of one country or of one area, even if important changes took place with the development of what he calls 'finance capitalism'. It was an aspect of the merchant economies that grew up with the Bronze Age, and even before. Once this has been recognized, the whole issue of the European (or even the English) miracle takes on a different form, as an aspect of interacting economies. Gone is the presumed advantage of antiquity, of feudalism, of capitalism, which supposedly characterized the west. And the east is no longer a slumbering giant (except at particular moments in time) but a participating partner, about to reclaim its former position. The alternative claim of the long-term advantage of Europe can be seen for what it was and is, the claim made by Europeans at the peak of their achievement in what has been an interactive process where east and west ran, by and large, parallel courses, without calling upon the idea of a sudden birth of 'capitalism' which privileged only the west. The west was, of course, privileged by the dramatic uptreaval that occurred in the eighteenth and nineteenth centuries, but that was but a temporary peak, not a permanent platform.

In the arts there is a kind of rough parity, or level-pegging as in the sciences. Of course, every culture will glorify its own, just as we do the Italian Renaissance. But China too has an on-going artistic tradition which is as much appreciated by its members. Expertise grew up in both east and west and was given expression in various forms, such as painting, the theatre and music.

That was the case in other spheres. One of the features of the period of internal alternation that we speak of as the Italian Renaissance was that it was not entirely internal, being influenced by outside powers, especially as trade built up with the east. One of its other advantages was that it freed some men from the restrictions that a hegemonic religion placed upon discovery about the world, freed scientists like Galileo to develop their speculation and to experiment with nature. Not that, in technology, invention was altogether absent before, especially in the water-driven agricultural machinery described in Agricola, or in the mines of central Europe where precious metals were sought, partly for export. This tradition existed in both east and west, with technology slowly improving its methods. The breakthrough to increased production came not so much with precious metals but with coal and iron, which formed the basis for the Industrial Revolution. However, this Revolution depended upon a series of deliberate, human-made, inventions, and these were effected by men who, like Galileo, had largely escaped from direct ecclesiastical interference and who reaped the benefits of the shift to secular, from transcendental, modes of thinking. Technology always had its own momentum, as it rarely challenged beliefs about the world, unlike astronomy. But sometimes it did, as with printing in Islam and the use of water mills in Ethiopia, or as with the restrictions on figurative representation throughout the Abrahamistic religions. But usually technologists could proceed where men of science feared to tread, until the Renaissance gave the latter a new and less fettered existence. The distinction between the two activities is sometimes a fragile one but it had meaning for the actors.

My thesis on alternation in Eurasia depends upon, first, the common origins of east and west in the Bronze Age of the Near East. Clearly, the east was more developed than Europe until Bronze Age people moved outside the Near East following the Greek invasions. But after that time there was constant interchange, as Braudel has shown well for the eastern Mediterranean. With the passage of time, societies in both areas tended to approximate to the same standards of living, exchanging many kinds of object as well as information. The result was that the written cultures tended to resemble one another, for example in features like cooking and the use of flowers, in opposition to the Neolithic societies of Africa and elsewhere. Within this broad comparability of cultures, there were of course plenty of differences. But there were also periods, with regard to science and technology (less so with art and 'culture'), when the east led the way, and others when the west did, whether it was inventing a new way of recording numbers or another method of smelting iron. These features swing back and forth, partly depending upon the balance of trade. The important point was that over the longer term, the various civilizations influenced by the Bronze Age were virtually at level pegging; there was temporary advantage, giving rise to an alternation but no permanent superiority of one over the other, as so much of history and social science assumes. But the standpoint of these fields is essentially that of the nineteenth century when the west had seized the high ground in the economy, in military matters, as in the knowledge society more generally.

Appendix 1
Arguments of the Europeanists

In chapter 1, I tried to modify 'essentialist' aspects of the miracle thesis. The authors of the conference papers later published in Baechler, Hall and Mann[1] were strongly opposed to this 'alternating' approach. Many of these authors supported the thesis, spelt out by Laslett,[2] that there was a 'remarkable difference between Europe and the rest of the world in matters of industry, commerce and perhaps political aggrandisement' (which he then attributed 'to some extent' to an entirely 'individual' family system). Laslett was one of those most committed to the idea of a European miracle, although in his case it was a north-western European one. He regarded the transformation as being related to an individual family[3] which, since he was thoroughly in agreement with the 'Hajnal line' concerning demographic variables, excludes Italy and Spain, where, in this view, early industrialization did not occur.[4] However, that is to exclude the great exploration activity of the latter, its seizure of bullion and the significance of Genoa in early financial activities, of which Burke writes approvingly (in Renaissance terms). And it is to exclude the whole of the mechanized silk-making production of Lucca, Bologna and Lyons, which assisted in the build-up of English industrial activity in the eighteenth century. For Laslett was concerned with the miracle of the English, which

Appendix 1

he linked with their 'individualistic' domestic pattern rather than considering the miracle as a European (and even less a Eurasian) phenomenon; the Italian Renaissance was not initially followed by comparable demographic changes to those that occurred in western Europe.

According to Laslett,[5] in Europe 'procreation was reserved to those successful enough under the prevalent economic circumstances to create their own households'. In Asia and Africa, 'where marriage was early and universal', procreation was not so restricted. Later marriage, in the main, was 'companionate', not arranged by the parents, dowries were relatively unimportant, the out-living children living independently and accumulating for themselves. And such independence gave rise to labour mobility, making easier the 'concentrations of industrial population'. Many even left for North America. The system, he argues, had 'an industrialistic, competitive, capitalistic character' which was 'quintessentially European'[6] and 'unique'. Nevertheless, it had a collective aspect, not only for family dependents but also in the (English) Poor Law. These features were particularly characteristic of north-west Europe, an area of 'maximum productive innovation' and the 'earliest industrialization'. This did not occur in Italy and Spain, which failed to display Hajnal's 'European Marriage Pattern' (of late marriage and service in neighbouring households), though Japan did.

Other contributors adapted the same general approach as Laslett, but his was profoundly ethnocentric. The Hajnal pattern applies to northern Europe, not to southern, but that is surely where European industrialization and mechanization began, in the paper and silk mills of Italy and Spain, not to speak of the Renaissance itself. This hypothesis only accounts for half of Europe and then for a late period, the eighteenth century. Moreover, the assumptions about the unique capitalist character of Europe are not justified by the evidence even if one accepts the narrow, nineteenth-century definition of 'capitalism'. And all the argument depends on that. Life-cycle service was certainly not unique in the west nor was the dowry unimportant, even for those without

Arguments of the Europeanists

prospects, for the church or charity might provide. However, later marriage did allow some greater choice of spouse. But class and property considerations were of the greatest importance, as any reader of Jane Austen will know. And while marriage was late, it was also 'fertile', especially as there was no post-partum taboo on sex.

Laslett saw this north-western European arrangement, in contrast to that of Asia and Africa (and of the south of the favoured continent), as capable of rectifying the imbalance between population and resources and as being more stable in the face of famine. Natural disasters, like the bubonic plague, did not have the same devastating effects as in those less happy situations; spare fertility could be brought into play.

The evidence for the comparative effects of the bubonic plague in Europe (England) and the Near East (and elsewhere) is very thin. Did the influenza epidemic differ greatly in its consequences in Asia and Europe, the former of which he saw as being 'administratively inefficient by contrast with the latter'? It needs pointing out again that the evidence for this statement is lacking, especially considering the early development of an elaborate bureaucracy in China well before this existed in western Europe. But China is nevertheless said to be the subject of 'acute crises of population' which Europe never had.[7] Nor did they have a family system of the European kind which taught the participants 'the necessity of saving'; a new Chinese couple did not have to set up an independent conjugal household, so there was not the same 'discipline' which Weber thought necessary for the development of capitalism. All this was ensured by later marriage (which was 'companionate' and made by the partners). Leaving aside the question of the age of marriage, the view that a new domestic couple in China did not save up for itself is contrary to the facts; for if you did not immediately found a separate dwelling, that did not mean that you did not look forward to your own hearth, within the same building (as I have long ago shown for the LoDagaa of northern Ghana[8]).

Appendix 1

The difference of Europe is even held to apply to insurrections, where those of western and central Europe are thought to 'contrast greatly with those of Russia'.[9] Predictably, those of Japan are secular,[10] as is the case with capitalistic achievement generally,[11] or with feudalism.[12] But, equally, China and India are held to differ from both Japan and Europe.[13] For only in Europe are the real communities to be found, constituting the basis of this typology of insurrection,[14] where people are 'grouped around a Protestant or Catholic church', constituting 'a moral, affective and political unit'. These made up autonomous decision-making bodies, unlike similar aggregations elsewhere, and are said to express basic European values.[15] These values were related to Christianity, which considers every human person to be of 'prime value' as manifested in the Rights of Man; again the contrast is drawn with Russia, with India and China. In this characterization, Pillorget apparently has not considered the influence of Buddhism in Asia, let alone the general considerations of the society, which would necessarily involve such values. This contrast he relates to the absence of monotheism (which in fact kept the west in chains for a long period of time). Nevertheless, Europe alone is characterized by a sense of justice and of liberty (which is said to stem from 'ownership'), in opposition to the Turks or the Russians. We had absolutism, they had tyranny, whereas China 'did not know this notion of law'.[16] This is not so much a characterization as a caricature.

The theme of the nature of the state is continued in Mutel's discussion of Japan, which rightly looks back beyond the Tokugawa period. However, in drawing attention to Japan, he also describes China as 'backward',[17] saying that, like Korea, it 'did not become modernised';[18] he even speaks of 'failure' in the case of China, a view which is hardly sustainable in the twenty-first century.

The looking-back to earlier laws in Japan emphasized that 'modernization' is rooted in the pre-modern, that we have a definite process of social evolution from earlier Bronze Age culture. But we also have periods of 'blockage' and, in the

118

European case, one has to see 'modernization' in the Renaissance and after as involving the overcoming of a certain blockage related to the dominant religion and the fall of Rome. Werner takes an opposite, and very much a Europeanist, view of development, which sees the germs of the 'miracle' as being located in a Christian world that looked back to Hebrew prophets, to the Greek *polis*, to Roman imperialism and to the Middle Ages – the complete genealogy of European culture. To regard this as a continuous, uninterrupted development seems quite contrary to the facts. The faith in Catholicism and in continuity even leads him to deny Le Goff's attempt to pin-point the doctrine of redemption as emerging in the twelfth century, as he traces it back to St Augustine,[19] who helped cut European Christianity off from the classical tradition. Werner speaks about the build-up of capital by the church, which produced a pot into which the powerful and entrepreneurs could dip. But in general the church took property out of circulation, so that legal restrictions had to be set against mortmain, which limited the land and capital under the 'dead hand' of the ecclesia. And in one sense 'capitalism' did not emerge until those lands were confiscated in England by Henry VIII, or in France under the French Revolution. The 'capitalism of prayers' was certainly in conflict with the capitalism of the entrepreneurs.

Christianity is also a relevant factor in the analysis of Macfarlane,[20] as well as of Pillorget.[21] Alan Macfarlane takes the same anglophile line as Laslett and asks: 'Why in western Europe should they (England) alone lead to the growth of capitalism?' The 'growth', note, not the origin. He sees this as relating to the 'substratum of feudalism' of the Germanic system and specifically its 'form of property': to 'internalized property based on the household'.[22] The emergence of capitalism in England 'required not only a particular geographical, religious and technological complex, but, above all, a particular politico-economic system',[23] namely feudalism, which he, like others, found difficult to define, but he resorts to Maitland and the lord–vassal relationship, and recognizes that in many ways the characteristics of feudalism are inimical to capitalism. In particular, it restricted economic freedom and lacked central control. But the English version of feudalism differed from the continental – and, in particular, from the French – in displaying an element of 'patrimonialism', of centralization, comparable to the historian Perry Anderson's 'absolutism'.

In his chapter, the editor, Mann, also places the emphasis on the difference back in the 'feudal' period where he sees the European's primary concern with 'a small group of peasants' 'intensively exploiting their own locality'.[24] Medieval agriculture 'fostered dynamism' and gave rise to an intellectual environment 'conducive to what was understood by natural sciences'. This, combined with a 'Christian achievement' (again), led to 'the creation of a minimal normative society', running across various boundaries. But it could well be argued that all agricultural societies centred around some type of village community: in east and south-east Asia, the village was based on a much more intensive rice-cultivation, with sometimes three crops a year, which Bray and Needham see as more dynamic than corn agriculture (though this existed in the north of the country).[25] The Christian achievement in producing a minimal normative society was certainly no greater than in Islam, which stretched from southern Spain to the margins of China. This Chinese society encouraged a natural science well before post-classical Europe. While early Christianity with its Abrahamistic monotheism may well have provided a sense of identity (what regime did not?), it did much to inhibit the intellectual enquiry that is necessary for 'natural science', in some places right up to the present day, for example with creationism; that was the role of hegemonic monotheism. For Christianity was not at first 'the transmitter . . . of the classical legacy'.[26] The pagan emphasis of the Renaissance made it dominantly so. Until then it denied much of its 'ancestry', intellectually and in figurative representation in painting and in drama. There seems to have been little special about Europe in these respects; how then was it any more 'dynamic' than other Eurasian cultures?

Arguments of the Europeanists

The sinologist Elvin, too, takes up the Chinese case, but in a very different way. He operates his explanation on the basis of a radical distinction 'between "pre-modern" and "modern" farming techniques (the main criterion being scientific and industrial inputs)'.[27] He argues that while, around 1800, China and Europe were not far apart in many respects, the Chinese machinery 'remain at the level of the artisan's intuitive adaptations'[28] rather than displaying the characteristics of machinery in Europe. The contrast is not present in medieval times but developed only later. The important aspect of Elvin's argument, apart from what I regard as the perhaps questionable nature of the hypothesis of the blockage due to the 'high-level equilibrium trap', is the nature of alternation between China and the west. At the same time, his reasons for the acknowledged European advance in later times seem too 'spiritual' and overgeneralized. The European profligacy with energy and materials had to do with available resources; certainly the availability of coal and iron were critical. But he also speaks of 'the flair for accuracy' (2) and 'a man of precisely visualized mechanical fantasy' (3). Finally he claims the Europeans developed an X-ray vision with regard to machines (4). This latter attempt to list their differences relates to attitudinal or psychological variables that seem very difficult to measure or to judge. But at least he puts the difference in terms of a recent alternation that recognized China's earlier advantage in developing mechanization and the division of labour, and in exporting a huge quantity of commodities. To describe this as pre-modern in contrast to the west's modernization seems quite arbitrary.

The general factor proposed by the three editors relates to the nature of the state system: the 'organic states' in Hall's phrase, feudalism and rent in Wickham's contribution. The feudal rent, rather than centralized taxation, is critical to the mode of production (he prefers the articulation of the modes of production to explanations in terms of the state). In Islam you had the Mamluks possibly constituting a blockage, as Garcin discusses, although preferring to talk in terms of the absence of resources, especially of wood and metal. It was

Appendix 1

the former approach looking to a Mamluks blockage, that Cook speaks of as the Dynorod model.[29]

Mann sees these features of the medieval economy as being 'explained' by the 'gradual growth of Iron Age peasant agriculture in areas that privileged "heavier soils" and open-sea navigation'. The advantages of the former seem to me open to question given the impressive nature of intensive agriculture in the east where so many of our fruit and flowers originate. And as for open sea navigation, this did not play much part in Europe until the Renaissance, whereas the activities of China, India and Islam in the east were impressive for the exchange of goods and information in the ocean area, at a much earlier time, as that merchant's guide, the *Periplus*, tells us. This was part of their eastward expansion which Mann looks upon, in Venetian and Byzantine terms, as an 'unproductive struggle'.[30] 'Unproductive' is hardly the epithet for a series of exchanges that gave us paper, the compass and gunpowder, not to speak of silk and cotton, of some mechanization and factory production and, I would argue, the basis of much capitalist and scientific activity. In this, the historians Braudel and Needham would agree, reserving for the west the advent of 'finance (or industrial) capitalism' and of 'modern science',[31] a re-assuringly European idea which is strongly challenged by the actual situation. No one wishes to deny Europe (or America) its recent advantage, only to dispute the reasons given which all too often relate to imaginary long-term superiority or even a uniqueness that is frequently of an essentialist kind. The advantages, however, are of much more recent and specific origin and less long-standing in nature, as I would suggest current developments – including the Olympic Games of 2008 and the Chinese space voyages (not to speak of their huge exports) – make clear. Mann sees European uniqueness as related to the 'universalistic, diffuse set of private property power relations we know as capitalism'.[32] It is true that we see the modern economy as marked by the concept and actuality of private property. This is what many scholars, including Marx and Anderson,[33] have supposed. It is part of the general view of society as developing from communal to private property arrangements. The latter have in some extensive ways (but not in others) come to predominate, but it is extravagant to claim that this arrangement did not exist before – of course it did. To think of our arrangements as necessarily more 'individualistic' is in some ways an error. McNeill writes that in a 'restless inability . . . lies the true uniqueness of western civilization',[34] but this might result in anarchy – though it did not.

Another editor, Hall, takes a similar view but brings in a comparative element in considering the data, including once again the importance of Christianity, not neglecting that of commerce and of a fragmented, non-bureaucratic political system. He contends that what was important was that in Europe no single empire existed (as in the case of China) but rather a multiplicity of states which provided for the auto-nomy of the market.[35] What was different from India and Islam, where you had fragmentation, was that in northern Europe you had the 'organic state' with its limit to arbitrari-ness. 'Christianity held Europe together' and you did not have 'a predatory or bureaucratic government' which was hostile to economic development. Market relations, he argues, require autonomy plus extensive networks.[36] In China you had the latter but not the former. In Islam and India the state was weak and short-lived. One saw economic progress when long-enduring states were forced to interact by military com-petition. But military competition also meant huge expendi-ture on arms, which China saved by having a centralized state. The argument here seems very much a case of special pleading.

My central disagreement has to do with the rise of some state of the world called 'capitalism'. That is to say, I see the bases of our present system as going back much further than is commonly supposed. It is clear that important changes took place when industrial production picked up in Europe, using steam and water power and iron technology. This led to the Industrial Revolution which gave Europe a distinct advantage – temporary, as is now clear, because in many ways the development originated elsewhere in Asia where it is now being taken up again. But to see a completely new mode of production being born in Europe in the sixteenth century – or for some earlier – seems to me a misunderstanding of world history.

It is then generally agreed that there was a system of proto-industrial production in India and China in the seventeenth and eighteenth centuries, that is, a system in its early phase.[37] Some economic historians explain the failure further to develop an industrial economy in exogenous terms, some in endogenous. The first group relate the problem to competition with Europe. The latter attach importance to the insecurity of the capital market, the lack of mobility of the labour force attached to the land or the family, and the concentration of a large part of a money surplus in the hands of a centralized, semi-theocratic monarchy.[38]

Clearly changes took place in Europe that enabled it:

1. to dominate the physical world from the late fifteenth century (with ships and guns and later aeroplanes and atomic bombs);
2. to dominate the world of knowledge from the sixteenth century (with the printing press), and later the world of media through the cinema and the political economy of worldwide distribution;
3. to dominate the world of manufacture from the late eighteenth century (with industrial production).

These achievements followed the pre-eminence of China and India in the Pacific, and the contribution of other Eurasian cultures to the growth of knowledge,[39] and the enormous exports of China and India. Moreover, the advantage of Europe was relatively short-lived. Even in the nineteenth century, America took on its share of manufacture, and later of the other related activities as well. But this was carried out by Europeans outside Europe.

Subsequent changes extended the breakthrough of the rest of the world.

Arguments of the Europeanists

1. With the large-scale abandonment of colonial rule in Africa in 1960, in Asia post-World War II, and in the Americas even before, political domination collapsed, although the idea of continuing economic domination is embodied in the new world order created by the victory in the Second World War, as well as in the notion of neo-colonialism.

2. The domination of manufacture has ended with the industrialization of Japan, of the gang of four in the Far East, of Brazil and elsewhere in South America, of South Africa and Israel, with development in China and India – all these developments coming to the fore in recent years (in the last two cases, one should say 'once again').

3. The western domination of the world of knowledge and of world culture persists in some respects but has been significantly loosened. Globalization is no longer exclusively westernization.

Achievement of a concrete kind certainly took place in these contexts. And they have been described in global terms. Marx saw it as the shift from feudalism to capitalism arising out of particular relations of class conflict; others have talked of the rise of the bourgeoisie, the decline of the gentry. Historians define it as the beginning of the 'modern period', political scientists as modernization replacing traditionalism. Everyone – nearly everyone – sees it as a radical break from the past, although many historians derive particular features from the background of the culture that predisposed western Europe to take this step. In other words, the development was written in its cultural genes. Such an approach is especially widespread among English historians who, while they may talk of the European miracle, usually view it as an English one – hence the factors they see as critical to these changes need to be searched for in the English past.

I suggest that very little predisposed a later England or Europe towards major advances in any of these fields (but there was, of course, something, which we have examined in chapter 8). The miracle was for the whole of Eurasia and followed originally from the Bronze Age achievements. Indeed, while the ultimate results were great, the initial advances were small. Take the domination of the world. Sometimes this is attributed to attitudinal changes following the Reformation, thereby dismissing the enormous exploratory achievements of the Catholic states. But long before even these voyages, the Indian Ocean was constantly traversed by Arab, Indian and Chinese traders, whose activities were quite as intrepid and daring as those of western 'explorers'. What they lacked were the manoeuvrable small boats, the instrumentation (including a certain type of mechanical 'clock') and the firearms that the Europeans had; in each case, the advances were not great compared with what had gone before – for example the clock's tick-tock mechanism. China was the home of gunpowder without the musket, printing without the press, and large boats but without adjustable sails.

While European scholars have hunted around for predisposing and active contributing factors for subsequent events, the fields of religion, politics, kinship and ideology have yielded little to suggest that Europe had any monopoly on the future destiny of the world. Quite the contrary, the achievements of the later Middle Ages were ones of catching up with the earlier Mediterranean as well as with the contemporary east, and then pushing forward. Therein perhaps lies a germ of an explanation. It has been argued that the invention and full development of the alphabet was possible only outside the major world civilizations of Mesopotamia and of Egypt, whose cultures depended so profoundly on the first, logographic, systems of writing. Equally, it has been suggested that human capacity for advance lay in our being a less specialized anthropoid. The facts behind these views of aspects of social and genetic evolution are for discussion. But it could be that the relative simplicity, even 'backwardness', of western Europe was the most important factor in enabling it to take a temporary lead in those developments described as the 'European miracle'. It had to catch up with its trading partners and, in so doing, gained an advantage. Alternation was the rule in Eurasia.

Appendix 2
Water in east and west

We have spoken of the significance of water in rain-fed agriculture in Europe as against irrigated agriculture in Asia, the former being associated with 'democracy', the latter with 'despotism'. Regarding these latter characterizations, democracy (consultation of the people) existed in Asia and, while irrigation often required a centralized organization, that was not always the case. Nor does central control equal despotism. But, apart from the political or agricultural aspects, there is also the question of water (like the wind or animal traction) as power, as substituting for human labour. The effects of the abundance of water power in Europe, with its fast-flowing streams, are obvious if one looks at the many villages where water power was used for driving textile or other machinery in the late eighteenth and nineteenth centuries. India, where cotton was cultivated, processed and exported in such large quantities, never made much use of water power for such production. But when the processing of cotton was taken up in England in the Industrial Revolution, in the eighteenth century, it was power-driven mechanization that counted, as it was with the reeling of silk. Of course, there were already weaving machines and these might be worked in factory-like conditions, in *karkhanas*. But the power was always human. When the main production of cotton goods was (temporarily) taken over by the west, this was produced in watermills, in much larger quantities, and at lower cost, then exported to the rest of the world. It could do so not because it first introduced cotton as a textile, or even the principle of mechanization, or yet that of larger-scale production, but because it harnessed the plentiful water power and had developed the necessary machines (first in an agricultural and mining context) to exploit it. This process itself did not particularly require a special incentive nor even much entrepreneurial skill; it required the utilization of water power for production, which was an altogether different process in Europe than in most of Asia, where its slower streams were used in other agricultural tasks, such as in filling tanks or irrigation channels.

When water power was available, we can see what happened in the silk industry. Even for hand-weaving, there were hold-ups at the level of reeling. One weaver took up the thread of several of those working on reeling the cocoons. The problem was first solved in China[40] by the invention of the multiple reeling machine, powered by water, which invention eventually made its way to Lucca and then to Bologna, and it led to the great expansion of the European industry.[41] Finally the secrets were stolen and taken to England, where in 1718 they were incorporated by the Lombe family of entrepreneurs into the Great Mill of Derby and formed part of the essential kit of the Industrial Revolution that developed in that country. For this purpose, water power was essential and was intrinsic to the first American textile mill later established, along English lines, in Slatersville, Rhode Island.

Even more significant was the example of the paper industry which was again an import from China through the Muslim world. The industry depended upon the plentiful use of water and was developed as early as the beginning of the Christian era. It diffused through central Asia and eventually reached Baghdad in the eighth century, leading to a rapid increase in the circulation of information on this cheap, widely available material for reproducing the written word. Water mills were constructed on the river Tigris for its production, which lay behind the translation movement from Greek to Arabic as well as the construction of a huge library – there, as elsewhere in the Islamic world, much larger than anything that then existed in Christian Europe. Paper was exported to that continent from the Near East and soon the technique of production was also transferred, first to Andalusia in southern Spain, and subsequently to Christian Spain and northern Italy, possibly from Muslim Salerno. There production expanded rapidly, and soon Europe had reversed the direction of imports and was exporting paper to the Near East. It could manufacture the material at lower cost because it could use the water of fast-flowing streams to work the mills. Water power was also used for mining metals and fast-working textile mills. The earlier availability and increased power of water enabled Europe to adopt a more efficient method of production, which reversed a measure of dependence on China and the Near East.

The geographer and historian Tony Wrigley has made a similar point regarding the use of fossil fuel, coal and peat, which is widely distributed in western Europe.[42] However, my argument is that it is not the use of a particular form of energy that gave rise to capitalism, in the west or anywhere else. Large-scale production developed in many parts with the use of non-human energy: in China with heat in the ceramic trade, which eventually gave rise to the production of Delft and Staffordshire, as well as with water power in silk textiles and in paper; in India, complex loom and spinning machines for cotton employed human labour but might also operate in large workshops or factories, as in Islam. Any machinery, any use of non-human labour, any cooperative activity, meant an intensification of commodity production, on which Marx placed so much emphasis. But he was mistaken in thinking this only happened in Europe. 'The circulation of commodities is the starting point of capital', he wrote of the late medieval period. But commodity production had

Appendix 2

started long before, with the development of trade. It is only by defining commodity and market exchange in a very restricted way that his formula for capitalism[43] can possibly work. If one is using the word for extensive commodity exchange, inevitably involving the accumulation of capital, then, as Braudel has said, capitalism is a widespread institution, having been practised early on in China, India and the Near East, to mention only the biggest players on the Eurasian continent.

Notes

1 ALTERNATION OR SUPREMACY

1 J. R. Goody 1982, 1993.

2 WHY EUROPEAN AND NOT EURASIAN?

1   J. R. Goody 1990.
2   Andreski 1983.
3   Mintz 1985: 58.
4   Bois 1984: 4.
5   In the works of the historian Polanyi, and the Orientalists Diakonof, Oppenheim, Larsen, Veenhof, Garelli and others.
6   Wheatley 1975.
7   E.g. studies by the Islamist, Rodinson.
8   Glick 1979: 6.
9   Especially in the works of the historians Postan, Duby and Stock.
10 Pearson 1976.
11 J. R. Goody 1979.
12 Raychaudhuri and Habib 1982: 314–15.
13 Raychaudhuri and Habib 1982: xiv.
14 Mintz 1985: 164.
15 Oppenheim 1964: 84.
16 Finley 1973: 74.

17 Whittaker and Goody 2001.
18 Pearson 1976: 29.
19 Rawson 1984.
20 Irwin and Brett 1970; Irwin and Hall 1971.
21 Raychaudhuri and Habib 1982: 400.
22 Lardinois 1986: 22; for a similar example from north India, see Stern 1982: 140.
23 Mote 1977: 199.
24 Chao 1964: 961.
25 Chao 1964: 683.

3 DOMESTIC ASPECTS OF THE 'MIRACLE'

1 J. R. Goody 1996b.
2 Malthus 1798.
3 J. R. Goody and Addo 1977.
4 For a European example of the latter, see Tindall 1995 on the recent history of the village of Chassingolles in the Berry, central France.
5 Chayanov 1986.
6 J. R. Goody 1996a.
7 J. R. Goody 1990; Hajnal 1982.
8 Bossy 1973: 130; Thomas 1971; Macfarlane 1978.
9 Bossy 1973: 131.
10 Sheehan 1971: 229.
11 Mann 1986.
12 Jones 1981.
13 Jones 1981: 13, my italics. But, of course, such extensive forms of agriculture were found in many other parts of the world and it is highly doubtful whether the practitioners can reasonably be said to be more 'individualist' in any overall sense than people with a more differentiated division of labour (indeed Durkheim's argument about mechanical and organic solidarity might suggest the opposite).
14 Jones 1981: 3.
15 Blaut 1993: 25.
16 Ikegami 1995: 330.
17 Ikegami 1995: 331, my italics.
18 Ikegami 1995: 350.
19 Ikegami 1995: 352.

20 J. R. Goody 1958.
21 Lee and Feng 1999: 81.
22 A. Wolf and Huang 1980.
23 Lee and Feng 1999: 106.
24 Lee and Feng 1999: 4.
25 Lee and Feng 1999: 4, my italics.
26 Lee and Feng 1999: 5.
27 Lee and Feng 1999: 9–10.
28 Lee and Feng 1999: 10, my italics.
29 Lee and Feng 1999: 10.
30 Lee and Feng 1999: 96.
31 Lee and Feng 1999: 9, my italics.
32 J. R. Goody 1996a.
33 Lee and Feng 1999: 12.
34 Lee and Feng 1999: 105.
35 By Wrigley and Schofield 1981: xxiv.
36 J. R. Goody 1983.
37 Lee and Feng 1999: 109.
38 Lee and Feng 1999: 111.
39 Lee and Feng 1999: 124.
40 Lee and Feng 1999: 125.
41 Lee and Feng 1999: 123.
42 Lee and Feng 1999: 21.
43 Lee and Feng 1999: 40.
44 Lee and Feng 1999: 135.
45 Lee and Feng 1999: 136.
46 Lee and Feng 1999: 140.
47 Lee and Feng 1999: 140.
48 Lee and Feng 1999: 145.
49 J. R. Goody 1990, 1996a.

4 EURASIA AND THE BRONZE AGE

1 Morgan 1877.
2 I was attracted to prehistory partly through living in St Albans where Mortimer Wheeler was then digging up the Neptune mosaic at Verulamium, partly through a mathematics master at school whose East Anglian heritage had made him very keen on Paleolithic Material. But above all my interest expanded when, during the Second World War, I travelled in the East and read

Gordon Childe's *What Happened in History*, a book that has always remained at the forefront of my thinking. My knowledge was broadened when I returned to Cambridge, read Archaeology and Anthropology, and met Dorothy Garrod, Graham Clarke and, above all, Glyn Daniel who was my supervisor. In what I want to say, I try to relate Childe's work to my own, with food as the background but taking in a wider perspective.

3   E. R. Wolf 1982.

4   J. R. Goody 2004.

5   Braudel 1981–4.

6   Poni 2001a and b.

7   J. R. Goody 1982.

8   J. R. Goody 1993.

9   Mexican cuisine possibly represents another form but I have confined my attention to Eurasia.

10   Clunas 1991.

11   Brook 1998.

12   Braudel 1981–4.

13   Speiser 1985.

14   Lane 1973.

15   Perera 1951, 1952a and b.

16   Sabloff and Lambeg-Karlowsky 1975; Leur 1955; Melink-Roelofsz 1962, 1970.

17   Goitein 1967.

18   Casson 1989, for the Periplus.

19   See also Mintz 1985.

20   Chang 1977.

21   China was not the beginning of restaurant culture. In the fourth millennium BCE archaeologists found buildings at Nimrod in Syria which have been interpreted as public eating places.

22   E.g. Poni 2001a and b.

23   See Poni 2001a and b; Goody 2004: 140.

24   Bray 2000: 1.

25   Bray 1997.

26   Ledderose 1992.

27   I am not aware that much is known about the production of food for these enterprises, but clearly they changed the patterns of consumption in substantial ways.

28   J. R. Goody 1996a: 187.

29   Mintz 1985.

5 MERCHANTS AND THEIR ROLE IN ALTERNATION

1 J. R. Goody 1972.
2 Kroeber 1953.
3 Larsen 1976.
4 Schmandt-Bessarat 1996.
5 See Clark 1961.
6 Renfrew 2007.
7 I reject entirely Polanyi and other theories of a pre-market economy, as in 'primitive communism'. They derive from a mistakenly utopian vision of the human past, and perhaps its future.
8 Ghosh 1992.
9 See Weber 1985. Only the west is supposed to have permitted the growth of 'capitalism'.
10 Wallerstein 1999.

6 MERCHANT WEALTH AND PURITANICAL ASCETICISM

1 Baechler, Hall and Mann 1988.
2 Proust 1924.
3 J. R. Goody 1997.
4 J. R. Goody 1993.
5 J. R. Goody 1982.
6 In J. R. Goody 1998.
7 Daniels 1995: 46.
8 Goody 1982.
9 Coldstream 1977: 25.
10 R. M. Cook 1960: 2.
11 Coldstream 1977: 71.
12 Coldstream 1977: 71.
13 R. M. Cook 1960: 4.

7 TOWARDS A KNOWLEDGE SOCIETY

1 Atkins 2004: 53.
2 See Renfrew 2007.
3 Lewis-Williams 2002.
4 J. R. Goody 1977.

5 J. R. Goody and Gandah 1980.
6 J. R. Goody and Gandah 2002.
7 Furet and Ozouf 1977.
8 Schmandt-Besserat 1996.
9 Gernet 2002.
10 See Francis 1950.

8 THE TEMPORARY ADVANTAGE IN ALTERNATION OF THE POST-RENAISSANCE WEST

1 Needham 1954–.
2 Ledderose 1992.
3 Elvin 1973.
4 See Green 2008.
5 See, for instance, Rawski 1979.
6 J. R. Goody 2009.
7 Landes 1998.
8 Rostow 1991.
9 J. R. Goody 1998: chapter 11.
10 Was Manchester the first in the United Kingdom to do without one?
11 See Spufford 2002.
12 Crossley 1981: 40.
13 Crossley 1981.
14 Needham 2004: 34.
15 Needham 2004: 218.

9 ALTERNATION IN EURASIA

1 E. R. Wolf 1982.
2 J. R. Goody 2006, 2009.

APPENDIX 1 ARGUMENTS OF THE EUROPEANISTS

1 Baechler, Hall and Mann 1988.
2 Laslett 1988: 234.
3 Laslett 1988: 234.
4 Laslett 1988: 240.

5   Laslett 1988: 237.
6   Laslett 1988: 238–9.
7   Laslett 1988: 237.
8   See J. R. Goody 1971.
9   Pillorget 1988: 209.
10 Pillorget 1988: 204–10.
11 Laslett 1988: 240.
12 Marx 1964; Bendix 1966 (Weber); Anderson 1974; and Macfarlane 1988: 193.
13 Pillorget 1988: 210.
14 Pillorget 1988: 211.
15 Pillorget 1988: 212.
16 Pillorget 1988: 214.
17 Mutel 1988: 150.
18 Mutel 1988: 157.
19 Werner 1988: 174.
20 Macfarlane 1988: 201.
21 Pillorget 1988: 213.
22 Macfarlane 1988: 186.
23 Macfarlane 1988: 196.
24 Mann 1988: 15.
25 Needham 2004: 21.
26 Mann 1988: 16.
27 Elvin 1988: 105.
28 Elvin 1988: 112.
29 Cook 1988: 132.
30 Mann 1988: 17.
31 J. R. Goody 2007.
32 Mann 1988: 15.
33 Anderson 1974.
34 McNeill 1963: 539, quoted approvingly by Mann 1988: 12.
35 In recognizing there is 'a measure of truth to crudely materialistic understandings of ideological power as well as neo-idealist ones', Hall generously calls attention to my account (Goody 1983) that centres upon 'the land hunger of the Catholic church'. While this is not the place to comment on the grave explanatory problems that many social scientists cause by attempting a 'crude' separation between materialist and idealist understandings, I need to add that I see nothing specifically 'European' in the desire of great organizations to acquire rights over land (or its product) in largely agricultural

societies. The Buddhists did just this in Sri Lanka, in India and in China. Without it, they would find it difficult to be great organizations.

36 Hall 1988: 34.
37 Devon 1984: 876.
38 Devon 1984: 877.
39 J. R. Goody 2009.
40 Elvin 1973.
41 Poni 2001a and b, Goody 2004.
42 Wrigley 1988.
43 A pejorative term for the economy first used by the nineteenth-century authors Arthur Young, Disraeli and Thackeray.

References

Agricola, G. 1950 (1556) *De re metallica*, ed. H. C. and L. H. Hoover. New York: Dover Publications

Anderson, P. 1974 *Passages from Antiquity to Feudalism*. London: Verso

Andreski, S. (ed.) 1983 *Max Weber on Capitalism, Bureaucracy and Religion: A Selection of Texts*. London: Allen & Unwin

Atkins, P. 2004 *Galileo's Finger: The Ten Great Ideas of Science*. Oxford: Oxford University Press

Bacon, F. 1995 (1620) *Novum organum*, trans. P. Urbach and J. Gibson. Chicago: Open Court

Baechler, J., Hall, J. A. and Mann, M. (eds.) 1988 *Europe and the Rise of Capitalism*. Oxford: Blackwell

Bendix, R. 1966 *Max Weber: An Intellectual Portrait*. London: Methuen

Benjamin, W. 2008 (1935) *The Work of Art in the Age of Mechanical Reproduction*, trans. J. A. Underwood. London: Penguin

Blaut, J. M. 1993 *The Colonizer's Model of the World: Geographical Diffusionism and Eurocentric History*. London: Guildford Press

Bloch, M. L. B. 1966 (1931) *French Rural History: An Essay on its Basic Characteristics*. London: Routledge & Kegan Paul

Bois, G. 1984 (1970) *The Crisis of Feudalism*. Cambridge: Cambridge University Press

Bossy, J. 1973 Blood and baptism: kinship, community and Christianity in Western Europe from the fourteenth to the seventeenth

References

centuries. In D. Baker (ed.), *Sanctity and Secularity: The Church and the World*. Cambridge: Cambridge University Press

Braudel, F. 1981–4 (1979) *Civilisation and Capitalism, 15th–18th Century*, vol. I: *The Structures of Everyday Life*; vol. II: *The Wheels of Commerce*; vol. III: *The Perspective of the World*. London: Phoenix Press

Bray, F. 1997 *Technology and Gender: Fabrics of Power in Late Imperial China*. Berkeley: University of California Press

2000 *Technology and Society in Ming China (1368–1644)*. Washington, DC: American Historical Society

Brook, T. 1998 *The Confusion of Pleasure: Commerce and Culture in Ming China*. Berkeley: University of California Press

Burke, P. 1988 Republics of merchants in early modern Europe. In J. Baechler, J. A. Hall and M. Mann (eds.), *Europe and the Rise of Capitalism*. Oxford: Blackwell

Casson, L. 1989 *The Periplus Maris Erythraei: Text with Introduction, Translation and Commentary*. Princeton: Princeton University Press

Chandra, S. 1982 *Medieval India: Society, the Jagirdari Crisis and the Village*. Delhi: Macmillan

Chang, K. C. (ed.) 1977 *Food in Chinese Culture: Anthropological and Historical Perspectives*. New Haven: Yale University Press

Chao, K. 1964 La production textile en Chine. *Annales E. S. C.* 39: 957–76

Chaudhuri, K. N. 1962 Foreign Trade. 1. European Trade with India. In T. Raychaudari and I. Habib (eds.), *The Cambridge Economic History of India*, vol. I: *c.1200–c.1750*. Cambridge: Cambridge University Press

Chayanov, A. V. V. 1986 *On the Theory of the Peasant Economy*. Manchester: Manchester University Press

Childe, V. G. 1939 *What Happened in History?* Harmondsworth: Penguin

Clark, G. 1961 *World Prehistory: An Outline*. Cambridge: Cambridge University Press

Clunas, C. 1991 *Superfluous Things: Material Culture and Social Status in Early Modern China*. Cambridge: Polity

Coldstream, J. N. 1977 *Geometric Greece*. London: E. Benn

Cook, M. 1988 Islam: A Comment. In J. Baechler, J. A. Hall and M. Mann (eds.), *Europe and the Rise of Capitalism*. Oxford: Blackwell

Cook, R. M. 1960 *Greek Painted Pottery*. London: Methuen

References

Cornford, F. M. 1923 *Greek Religious Thought from Homer to the Age of Alexander*. London: J. M. Dent

Crossley, D. W. 1981 Medieval iron smelting. In D. W. Crossley (ed.), *Medieval Industry*, Research Report 40. London: Council for British Archaeology

Daniels, B. C. 1995 *Puritans at Play: Leisure and Recreation in Colonial New England*. Basingstoke: Macmillan

Derrida, J. 1974 *Of Grammatology*, trans. G. Spivak. Baltimore: Johns Hopkins University Press

1978 *Writing and Difference*, trans. A. Bass. London: Routledge & Kegan Paul

Devon, P. 1984 Fecondité et limites du model proto-industriel: premier plan. *Annales E. S. C.* 39: 861–81

Duby, G. 1968 *Rural Economy and Country Life in the Medieval West*, trans. C. Postan. London: Edward Arnold

Dumont, L. 1970 *Homo Hierarchicus: The Caste System and its Implications*, trans. M. Sainsbury. London: Weidenfeld and Nicolson

1977 *From Mandeville to Marx: The Genesis and Triumph of Economic Ideology*. Chicago: University of Chicago Press

Durkheim, E. 1933 (1893) *The Division of Labour in Society*, trans. G. Simpson. New York: The Free Press

Durkheim, E. and Mauss, M. 1963 (1903) *Primitive Classification*, trans. R. Needham. London: Cohen & West

Elias, N. 1994 (1978) *The Civilizing Process*. Oxford: Blackwell

Elvin, M. 1973 *The Pattern of the Chinese Past*. London: Eyre Methuen

1988 China as a counterfactual. In J. Baechler, J. A. Hall and M. Mann (eds.), *Europe and the Rise of Capitalism*. Oxford: Blackwell

Engels, F. 1972 (1884) *The Origin of the Family, Private Property and the State: In the Light of the Researches of Lewis H. Morgan*. London: Lawrence and Wishart

Evans-Pritchard, E. E. 1940 *The Nuer*. Oxford: Clarendon Press

Finley, M. 1973 *The Ancient Economy*. London: Chatto & Windus

Fortune, R. 1987 (1847) *Three Years' Wandering in the Northern Provinces of China, A Visit to the Tea, Silk, and Cotton Countries, with an account of the Agriculture and Horticulture of the Chinese, New Plants, etc*. London: Mildmay

References

Francis, J. de 1950 *Nationalism and Language Reform in China*. Princeton: Princeton University Press

Furet, F. and Ozouf, J. 1977 *Lire et écrire, l'alphabétisation des français de Calvin à Jules Ferry*. Paris: Minuit

Garcin, J.-C. 1988 The Mamlūk military system and the blocking of medieval society. In J. Baechler, J. A. Hall and M. Mann (eds.), *Europe and the Rise of Capitalism*. Oxford: Blackwell

Garelli, P. 1969 *Le Proche-Orient asiatique: des origines aux invasions des peuples de la mer*. 2 vols. Paris: Presses Universitaires de France

Gernet, J. 2002 (1982) *A History of Chinese Civilisation*, rev. 2nd edn, trans. J. R. Foster and C. Hartman. Cambridge: Cambridge University Press

Ghosh, A. 1992 *In an Antique Land*. New York: Vintage Books

Glick, T. F. 1979 *Islamic and Christian Spain in the Early Middle Ages: Comparative Perspectives on Social and Cultural Formation*. Princeton: Princeton University Press

Goitein, S. D. 1967 *Mediterranean Society: The Jewish Communities of the Arab World as Portrayed in the Documents of the Cairo Geniza*, vol. I. Berkeley, CA: University of California Press
1999 *Mediterranean Society: An Abridgement in One Volume*. Berkeley, CA: University of California Press

Goody, E. 1983 Introduction. In E. Goody (ed.), *From Craft to Industry: The Ethnology of Proto-industrial Cloth Production*. Cambridge: Cambridge University Press

Goody, J. R. (ed.) 1958 *The Developmental Cycle In Domestic Groups*. Cambridge: Cambridge University Press
1962 *Death, Property and the Ancestors*. Stanford: Stanford University Press
1971 The evolution of the family. In P. Laslett and R. Wall (eds.), *Household and Family in Past Time*. Cambridge: Cambridge University Press
(ed.) 1972 *The Myth of the Bagre*. Oxford: Clarendon Press
1977 *The Domestication of the Savage Mind*. Cambridge: Cambridge University Press
1979 Slavery in time and space. In J. L. Watson (ed.), *Asian and African Systems of Slavery*. Oxford: Blackwell
1982 *Cooking, Cuisine and Class*. Cambridge: Cambridge University Press
1983 *The Development of the Family and Marriage in Europe*. Cambridge: Cambridge University Press

References

1990 *The Oriental, the Ancient and the Primitive: Systems of Marriage and the Family in the Pre-industrial Societies of Eurasia.* Cambridge: Cambridge University Press

1993 *The Culture of Flowers.* Cambridge: Cambridge University Press

1996a *The East in the West.* Cambridge: Cambridge University Press

1996b Comparing family systems in Europe and Asia: are there different sets of rules? *Population and Development Review* 22: 1–20

1997 *Representations and Contradictions.* Oxford: Blackwell

1998 *Food and Love.* London: Verso

2004 *Capitalism and Modernity: The Great Debate.* Cambridge: Polity

2006 *The Theft of History.* Cambridge: Cambridge University Press

2009 *Renaissances: The One or the Many?* Cambridge: Cambridge University Press

Goody, J. R. and Addo, N. 1977 *Siblings in Ghana*, Population Studies, 7. Legon, Ghana: University of Ghana Press

Goody, J. R. and Braimah, J. A. 1967 *Salaga: The Struggle for Power.* London: Longmans

Goody, J. R. and Gandah, S. W. D. K. (eds.) 1980 *Une Récitation du Bagré.* Paris: Colin

(eds.) 2002 *The Third Bagre: A Myth Revisited.* Durham, NC: Carolina Academic Press

Goody, J. R. and Watt, I. 1963 The consequences of literacy. *Comparative Studies in Society and History* 5: 304–45

Gough, K. 1979 *Dravidian Kinship and Modes of Production.* The Irawati Karve Memorial Lecture for 1978. New Delhi: Indian Council of Social Science Research

1982 *Rural Society in Southeast India.* Cambridge: Cambridge University Press

Granet, M. 1958 *Chinese Civilization.* New York: Meridian

Green, A. 2008 The British Empire and the Jews: an imperialism of human rights? *Past and Present* 199: 175–205

Hajnal, J. 1982 Two kinds of pre-industrial household formation system. *Population and Development Review* 8: 449–94

Hall, J. A. 1985a Religion and the rise of capitalism. *Archives Européennes de Sociologie* 26: 193–223

References

1985b *Powers and Liberties: The Causes and Consequences of the Rise of the West*. Berkeley, CA: University of California Press

1988 States and societies: the miracle in comparative perspective. In J. Baechler, J. A. Hall and M. Mann (eds.), *Europe and the Rise of Capitalism*. Oxford: Blackwell

Harrison, J. E. 1912 *Themis*. Cambridge: Cambridge University Press

Hart, K. 1982 *The Political Economy of West Africa*. Cambridge: Cambridge University Press

Hill, P. 1970 *The Migrant Cocoa-farmers of Southern Ghana: A Study in Rural Capitalism*. Cambridge: Cambridge University Press

Hodges, R. and Whitehouse, D. 1983 *Mohammed, Charlemagne, and the Origins of Europe*. Ithaca: Cornell University Press

Ikegami, E. 1995 *The Taming of the Samurai: Honorific Individuals and the Making of Modern Japan*. Cambridge, MA: Harvard University Press

Irwin, J. and Brett, K. B. 1970 *The Origin of Chintz*. London: H.M.S.O.

Irwin, J. and Hall, M. 1971 *Indian Painted and Printed Fabrics*. Ahmedabad: Calico Museum of Textiles

Jardine, L. 1996 *Worldly Goods: A New History of the Renaissance*. London: Macmillan

Jones, E. L. 1981 *The European Miracle: Environments, Economics, and Geopolitics*. Cambridge: Cambridge University Press

Karageorghis, V. 1989 *The Cyprus Museum*, trans. A. H. and S. Foster Kromholz. Nicosia: C. Epiphaniou

Kroeber, A. L. 1953 *Handbook of Indians of California*. Berkeley, CA: California Book Company

Landes, D. 1998 *The Wealth and Poverty of Nations: Why Some Are So Rich and Some So Poor*. New York: Norton

Lane, F. C. 1973 *Venice: A Maritime Republic*. Baltimore: Johns Hopkins University Press

Lardinois, R. 1986 En Inde, la famille, l'État, la femme. In A. Burguière et al. (ed.), *Histoire de la famille*, vol. II. Paris

Larsen, M. T. 1976 *The Old Assyrian City-State and its Colonies*. Copenhagen: Akademisk Forlag

Laslett, P. 1988 The European family and early industrialization. In J. Baechler, J. A. Hall and M. Mann (eds.), *Europe and the Rise of Capitalism*. Oxford: Blackwell

References

Ledderose, L. 1992 Module and mass production. In *Proceedings of the International Colloquium on Chinese Art History, 1991, Painting and Calligraphy*, Part 2. Taiwan: National Palace Museum

Lee, J. Z. and Feng, Wang 1999 *One Quarter of Humanity: Malthusian Mythology and Chinese Reality*. Cambridge, MA: Harvard University Press

Le Goff, J. 1981 *La naissance du Purgatoire*. Paris: Gallimard

Leur, J. C. van 1955 *Indonesian Trade and Society: Essays in Asian Social and Economic History*, trans. J. S. Holmes and A. van Marle. The Hague: W. Van Hoeve

Lévi-Strauss, C. 1949 *Les structures élémentaires de la parenté*. Paris: Presses Universitaires de France

Lewis-Williams, D. 2002 *The Mind in the Cave*. London: Thames and Hudson

Loeb, J., et al. (ed.) 1912– *The Loeb Classical Library*. Cambridge, MA: Harvard University Press

Macfarlane, A. 1978 *The Origins of English Individualism*. Oxford: Blackwell

1988 The cradle of capitalism: the case of England. In J. Baechler, J. A. Hall and M. Mann (eds.), *Europe and the Rise of Capitalism*. Oxford: Blackwell

Maimon, S. 1954 *The Autobiography of Solomon Maimon*, trans. J. C. Murray. London: The East and West Library

Maimonides, M. 1963 *The Guide of the Perplexed*, trans. S. Pines. Chicago: University of Chicago Press

Maitland, F. W. 1919 *The Constitutional History of England*. Cambridge: Cambridge University Press

Malinowski, B. 2002 (1923) *Argonauts of the Western Pacific: An Account of Native Enterprise and Adventure in the Archipelagos of Melanesian New Guinea*. London: Routledge

Malthus, T. R. 1798 *An Essay on the Principle of Population*. London: J. Johnson

Mann, M. 1986 *The Sources of Social Power*, vol. II: *A History of Power from the Beginning to A.D. 1760*. Cambridge: Cambridge University Press

1988 European development: approaching a historical explanation. In J. Baechler, J. A. Hall and M. Mann (eds.), *Europe and the Rise of Capitalism*. Oxford: Blackwell

Marx, K. 1964 *Pre-capitalist Economic Formations*, trans. Jack Cohen, ed. E. Hobsbawm. London: Lawrence & Wishart

References

McNeill, W. 1963 *The Rise of the West: A History of the Human Community*. Chicago: University of Chicago Press

Meilink-Roelofsz, H. A. P. 1962 *Asian Trade and European Influence in the Indonesian Archipelago between 1500 and about 1630*. The Hague: Nijhoff

1970 Asian trade and Islam in the Malay–Indonesian archipelago. In D. S. Richards (ed.), *Islam and the Trade of Asia*. Oxford: B. Cassirer

Mintz, S. W. 1959 Labour and sugar in Puerto Rico and in Jamaica, 1800–1850. *Comparative Studies in Society and History* 1: 273–81.

1985 *Sweetness and Power: The Place of Sugar in Modern History*. New York: Viking

Morgan, L. H. 1877 *Ancient Society*. New York: Henry Holt

Mote, F. W. 1977. Yuan and Ming. In K. C. Chang (ed.), *Food in Chinese Culture: Anthropological and Historical Perspectives*. New Haven: Yale University Press

Mutel, J. 1988 The modernization of Japan: why has Japan succeeded in its modernization? In J. Baechler, J. A. Hall and M. Mann (eds.), *Europe and the Rise of Capitalism*. Oxford: Blackwell

Needham, J. (ed.) 1954– *Science and Civilization in China*. Cambridge: Cambridge University Press

1958 *The Development of Iron and Steel Technology in China*. London: Newcomen Society

2004 General conclusions and reflections. In K. G. Robinson (ed.), *Science and Civilization in China, Pt 2*, vol. VII. Cambridge: Cambridge University Press

Nicholas, D. 1985 *The Domestic Life of a Medieval City: Women, Children and the Family in Fourteenth-century Ghent*. Lincoln: University of Nebraska Press

Oppenheim, A. L. 1964 *Ancient Mesopotamia: Portrait of a Dead Civilization*. Chicago: University of Chicago Press

Parsons, T. and Bales, R. F. 1955 *Family, Socialization and Interaction Process*. Glencoe: Free Press

Pearson, M. N. 1976 *Merchants and Rulers in Gujerat: The Response to the Portuguese in the Sixteenth Century*. Berkeley, CA: University of California Press

Perera, B. J. 1951 The foreign trade and commerce of ancient Ceylon. I: The ports of ancient Ceylon. *Ceylon Historical Journal* 1: 109–19

References

1952a The foreign trade and commerce of ancient Ceylon. II: Ancient Ceylon and its trade with India. *Ceylon Historical Journal* 1: 192–204

1952b The foreign trade and commerce of ancient Ceylon. III: Ancient Ceylon's trade with the empires of the eastern and western worlds. *Ceylon Historical Journal* 1: 301–20

Petronius Arbiter 1996 *The Satyricon: Dinner with Trimalchio*. trans. R. Bracht Branham and D. Kinney. London: Phoenix

Pillorget, R. 1988 The European tradition in movements of insurrection. In J. Baechler, J. A. Hall and M. Mann (eds.), *Europe and the Rise of Capitalism*. Oxford: Blackwell

Pirenne, H. 1968 (1937) *Mohammed and Charlemagne*, trans. B. Miall. London: Allen & Unwin

Polanyi, K., et al. 1957 *Trade and Market in the Early Empires*. Glencoe: Free Press

Polo, M. 1968 *Travels of Marco Polo*, trans. R. Latham. London: Folio Society

Poni, C. 2001a Il *network* della setta nelle città italiana in età moderna. *Iscuola Officina* 2: 4–11

2001b Comparing two urban industrial districts: Bologna and Lyon in the early modern period. In P. P. Porta, R. Scazzieri and A. Skinner (eds.), *Knowledge, Social Institutions and the Division of Labour*. Cheltenham: Edward Elgar

Postan, M. 1932–4 Medieval capitalism. *Economic History Review* 4: 212–27

Proust, M. 1924 *La prisonnière*. Paris: Nouvelle Revue Française

Rawski, E. S. 1979 *Education and Popular Literacy in Ch'ing China*. Ann Arbor: University of Michigan Press

Rawson, J. 1984. *Chinese Ornament: The Lotus and the Dragon*. London: British Museum

Raychaudhuri, T. 1962 *Jan Company in Coromandel 1605–1690: A Study in the Interrelations of European Commerce and Traditional Economics*. The Hague: Nijhoff

Raychaudhuri, T. and Habib, I. (eds.) 1982 *The Cambridge Economic History of India*, vol. I: *c.1200–c.1750*. Cambridge: Cambridge University Press

Renfrew, C. 2007 *Prehistory: The Making of the Human Mind*. London: Weidenfeld and Nicolson

Ritter, G. A. 2000 *Continuity and Change: Political and Social Development in Germany after 1945 and 1989/90*, The 1999 Annual Lecture. London: German Historical Institute

References

Rodinson, M. 1949 Recherches sur les documents arabes relatifs à la cuisine. *Revue Études Islamiques* 17: 95–106
1973 *Islam and Capitalism*, trans. B. Pearce. New York: Pantheon Books
Rostow, W. W. 1991 (1960) *The Stages of Economic Growth*. Cambridge: Cambridge University Press
Sabloff, J. A. and Lambeg-Karlowsky, C. C. (eds.) 1975 *Ancient Civilization and Trade*. Albuquerque: University of New Mexico Press
Schmandt-Besserat, D. 1996 *How Writing Came About*. Austin: University of Texas Press
Sheehan, M. N. 1971 The formation and stability of marriage in fourteenth-century England: the evidence of an Ely Register. *Medieval Studies* 33: 228–63
Sheth, C. B. 1953 *Jainism in Gujarat*. Poona: Deccan College
Smith, A. 1895 (1776) *An Inquiry into the Nature and Causes of the Wealth of Nations*, ed. J. Nicholson. London: T. Nelson & Sons
Sombart, W. 1930 Capitalism. In *Encyclopedia of the Social Sciences*, vol. III. New York: Macmillan
Speiser, J. M. 1985 Le christianisation de la ville dans l'Antiquité tardive. *ktema: civilisations de l'orient, de la Grèce et de Rome antiques* 10: 49–55
Spencer, H. 1876–96 *The Principles of Sociology*, 3 vols. London: Williams and Norgate
Spufford, P. 2002 *Power and Profit: The Merchant in Medieval Europe*. London: Thames and Hudson
Steensgaard, N. 1974 *The Asian Trade Revolution of the Seventeenth Century: The East India Companies and the Decline of the Caravan Trade*. Chicago: University of Chicago Press
Stern, H. 1982 L'édification d'un secteur économique moderne: l'exemple d'une caste marchande du Rajasthan. *Purusartha* 6: 135–57
Stock, B. 1983 *The Implications of Literacy: Written Languages and Models of Interpretation in the Eleventh and Twelfth Centuries*. Princeton: Princeton University Press
Thomas, K. 1971 *Religion and the Decline of Magic*. London: Weidenfeld & Nicolson
Tindall, G. 1995 *Célestine: Voices from a French Village*. London: Sinclair-Stevenson

References

Todd, E. 1985 *The Explanation of Ideology: Family Structures and Social Systems*, trans. D. Garrioch. Oxford: Blackwell

Tylor, E. B. 1871 *Primitive Culture: Researches into the Development of Mythology, Philosophy, Religion, Art, and Custom*. London: John Murray

Veenhof, K. R. 1972 *Aspects of Old Assyrian Trade and its Terminology*, Studia et Documenta ad Iura Orientis Antiqui Pertinentia 10. Leiden: E. J. Brill

Vygotsky, L. S. 1978 *Mind in Society: The Development of Higher Psychological Processes*, trans. M. Cole. Cambridge, MA: Harvard University Press

Wallerstein, I. 1999 The west, capitalism and the modern world system. In T. Brook and G. Blue (eds.), *China and Historical Capitalism*. Cambridge: Cambridge University Press

Weber, M. 1985 (1905) *The Protestant Ethic and the Spirit of Capitalism*, trans. T. Parsons. London: Unwin

Wedgwood, J. 1929 *The Economics of Inheritance*. London: G. Routledge & Sons

Werner, K. F. 1988 Political and social structures of the West. In J. Baechler, J. A. Hall and M. Mann (eds.), *Europe and the Rise of Capitalism*. Oxford: Blackwell

Wheatley, P. 1961 *The Golden Khersonese: Studies in the Historical Geography of the Malay Peninsula before A. D. 1500*. Kuala Lumpar: University of Malaya Press

1975 Satyānṛta in Suvarṇadvīpa: from reciprocity to redistribution in ancient Southeast Asia. In J. A. Sabloff and C. C. Lamberg-Karlovsky (eds.), *Ancient Civilization and Trade*. Albuquerque: University of New Mexico Press

Whittaker, C. R. and Goody, J. R. 2001 Rural manufacturing in the Rouergue from Antiquity to the present: the examples of pottery and cheese. *Comparative Studies in Society and History* 43: 225–45

Wickham, C. 1988 The uniqueness of the East. In J. Baechler, J. A. Hall and M. Mann (eds.), *Europe and the Rise of Capitalism*. Oxford: Blackwell

Wolf, A. and Huang, C. 1980 *Marriage and Adoption in China, 1845–1945*. Stanford: Stanford University Press

Wolf, E. R. 1982 *Europe and the Peoples without History*. Berkeley, CA: University of California Press

References

Wrigley, E. A. 1988 *Continuity and Change: The Character of the Industrial Revolution in England*. Cambridge: Cambridge University Press

Wrigley, E. A. and Schofield, R. S. 1981 *The Population History of England, 1580–1837*. Cambridge: Cambridge University Press

Index

Index

Index

Index

Hinduism 9, 75, 87, 101,
109
Holland 75, 102
Homer 82, 88
Homo sapiens 22, 79, 80
human revolution 80, 81
humanism 12, 103, 104
hunter-gatherer societies 58,
95

iconophobia 70, 71, 72, 74
independent invention 50,
62
India 12, 89, 92, 98, 99, 110,
111, 118, 123
art 73
caste system 7, 14, 15, 16,
99
colonial 9
economy 13, 14, 16–17
education 101, 107
manufacturing 13–14, 15,
16, 54, 64, 110, 127,
129
mercantile activity 13–14
and modernization 107
proto-industrial production
13–14, 124
religion 99
trade 10, 14, 15, 16, 60, 61,
95
writing systems 88
individualism 7, 20, 25, 26,
27–32, 39
and eastern cultures 31, 32,
33–4, 35, 36, 39
economic 27, 29
emergence and diffusion of
27–8, 30, 31, 40
familial aspect 28, 29, 33–4,
36–7

'honorific' 32
political aspect 28–9, 32
possessive 32
rationality and 29, 32
religious 28, 30
western context 27–31, 32,
34, 35, 36, 37
individualism–collectivism
binary 33–4, 35, 36, 38,
39, 40
Indo-Europeans 30
Industrial Revolution 1, 2, 19,
63, 95, 97, 100, 103, 104,
113, 127, 128
roots of 111, 123
industrialization 2, 11, 17, 29,
44, 49, 116, 123
Asian proto-industrialism
13–14, 124
insurrections, typology of
118
Iraq 101
iron production and
ironworking 45, 103–4,
109, 113
irrigation 29, 30, 42, 127
Islam 9, 12, 41, 45, 66, 87,
92, 98, 99, 109, 113, 120,
121, 123
art 72–3
dominance of Mediterranean
trade 49
madrasas 100
and the printed word 92
puritanism 72–3
scientific scholarship
82–3
Italy 15, 19, 43, 44, 51, 64,
100–1, 115, 116, 129
see also Rome, Roman
Empire

155

Index

Index